Dreams of the Good Life

The Life of Flora Thompson and the Creation of Lark Rise to Candleford

RICHARD MABEY

ALLEN LANE
an imprint of
PENGUIN BOOKS

ALLEN LANE

Published by the Penguin Group

Penguin Books Ltd, 80 Strand, London WC2R ORL, England

Penguin Group (USA) Inc., 375 Hudson Street, New York, New York 10014, USA

Penguin Group (Canada), 90 Eglinton Avenue East, Suite 700, Toronto, Ontario, Canada M4P 2Y3
(a division of Pearson Canada Inc.)

Penguin Ireland, 25 St Stephen's Green, Dublin 2, Ireland (a division of Penguin Books Ltd)

Penguin Group (Australia), 707 Collins Street, Melbourne, Victoria 3008,
Australia (a division of Pearson Australia Group Pty Ltd)

Penguin Books India Pvt Ltd, 11 Community Centre, Panchsheel Park, New Delhi – 110 017, India

Penguin Group (NZ), 67 Apollo Drive, Rosedale, Auckland 0632, New Zealand
(a division of Pearson New Zealand Ltd)

Penguin Books (South Africa) (Pty) Ltd, Block D, Rosebank Office Park, 181 Jan Smuts Avenue,
Parktown North, Gauteng 2193, South Africa

Penguin Books Ltd, Registered Offices: 80 Strand, London WC2R ORL, England

www.penguin.com

First published 2014
001

Set in Dante 12/14.75pt. Typeset by Palimpsest Book Production Ltd, Falkirk, Stirlingshire
Printed in Great Britain by Clays Ltd, St Ives plc

ISBN: 978–1–846–14278–9

www.greenpenguin.co.uk

For Richard and Rose, our beacons in the Flatlands

Contents

Acknowledgements

Writing about a person as private as Flora Thompson, who lived most of her life some way outside the chattering world of mainstream literature, raises particular problems for a biographer. The usual reference sources are meagre in the extreme. Little of her correspondence survives, and her life – even when she had become a professional writer – passed almost unremarked by her literary contemporaries. So I am hugely grateful to those early researchers and writers who did the hard graft of burrowing in archives and record offices to put together the outlines of Flora's life: Margaret Lane, whose essay of 1957 was the first short biographical sketch; Gillian Lindsay for her more exhaustive study in 1990, written when there were still people alive with personal memories of Flora Thompson; Christine Bloxham, who has uncovered fascinating details about Flora's family and relatives; John Owen Smith, editor and publisher, who has done so much to bring Flora's unpublished manuscripts and unanthologized journals into book form; and Ruth Collette Hoffman, for her rigorous analysis and categorization of the whole body of Flora's work (full details of their books are in the Sources section at the end of the book).

Special thanks are due to the late Anne Mallinson, who first introduced me to Flora Thompson's work back in the 1970s, and who was a pioneer in championing Flora's work; and to Adam Freudenheim, late of Penguin, who originally commissioned this biography. Friends and colleagues who have provided source material, insights, wisdom and companionship on field-trips, include Ronald Blythe, Jon Cook, Gill Mabey, Robert Macfarlane, Leo Mellor, the late Richard Simon, Sean Street and Gavin Weightman. Thanks also to the Bodleian Library, the Oxfordshire County Record Office and the Castle Museum, Buckingham. My agent Vivien Green and my publisher / editor at Penguin, Helen Conford, kept faith with the book and helped to re-set the book's compass after a rather erratic first draft. Jane Robertson's copy-editing was diligent beyond the call of duty, especially with my fallible transcriptions, and Stephen Ryan was a meticulous proof-reader. Polly, as always, endured the trials of being a writer's partner with immense patience and kept my confidence afloat at those inevitable times when I imagined the book to be in danger of sinking.

Most of all I must thank three people: Alexandra Harris for her insightful remarks about cultural life in the inter-war years and, in the gentlest of ways, for pointing out instances of thoughtless male bias in the writing; Rose Tremain for a stray remark she made about the business of characterization in fiction, which she won't remember but which opened up a whole new perspective on Flora's work; and finally to Richard Holmes for his support and wise counsel throughout the writing of the book, and at the end for an act of extraordinary friendship and generosity: turning a somewhat muddled, apologetic first draft into a real narrative by an act of literary origami. He refolded my material into a different shape with the loss of only a few of my original pages. Any remaining infelicities are mine alone, and to him and Rose this book is dedicated.

For permission to use copyright material, I am enormously grateful to John Owen Smith and Gillian Lindsay for allowing me to use freely material from their books; to the Harry Ransom

Center, the University of Texas at Austin, for permission to use extracts from documents in their Flora Thompson archives and for making them available to me in digital form; to Elizabeth Swaffield and the Flora Thompson Estate for permission to quote from copyright material; and to the Oxford University Press for permission to use extracts from *Lark Rise to Candleford*. The extract from 'The South Country' from *Complete Verse* by Hilaire Belloc (Gerald Duckworth & Co., 1970) is reprinted by permission of Peters Fraser and Dunlop (www. petersfraserdunlop.com) on behalf of the Estate of Hilaire Belloc.

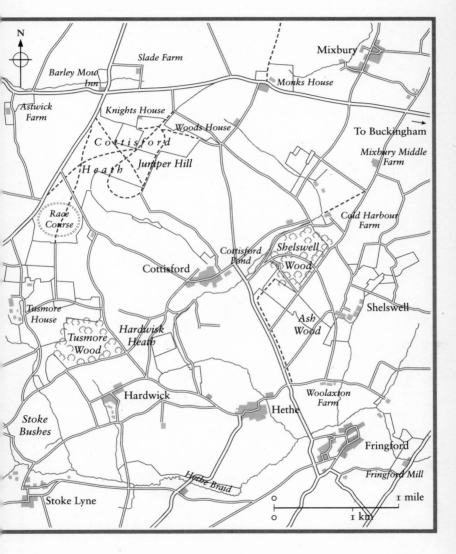

The countryside around Flora's home in Juniper Hill, Oxfordshire,
late nineteenth century

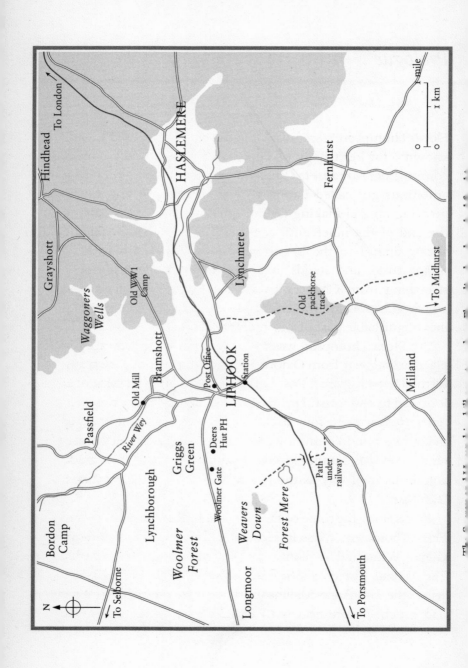

The Surrey–Hampshire–Sussex borders. Drawn by Mark Vine.

Prologue

Flora Thompson (1876–1947) is best known – perhaps only known – for her trilogy of books about life in the Victorian countryside, *Lark Rise to Candleford*. It's the story of a poor but ambitious girl called Laura (a version of her younger self) growing up and making do in a small Oxfordshire village at the end of the nineteenth century. The book has retained a strong appeal to the persistent British fascination with all things rural, and stands in a long and eclectic tradition – stretching from Chaucer to Ronald Blythe's *Akenfield* – in which affection for the countryside seems an essential and inextinguishable part of our national identity.

But Flora Thompson was to live for another half-century in places a long way from Oxfordshire, and during this time transformed herself from a Post Office clerk who had left school at fourteen to a successful professional writer. *Lark Rise* was written retrospectively, four decades later, when the author was living two hundred miles west of her Oxfordshire birthplace. Her career was another kind of rural achievement, as remarkable in its own way as the heroic survivals she celebrates in *Lark Rise*.

It was along the route of her travels west that I first discovered Flora Thompson. I was in Hampshire, working on a study of Gilbert White and his pioneering book of ecology and rural life, *The Natural History of Selborne*. Selborne's enterprising bookseller, the late Anne Mallinson (who, with hindsight, I fancy had much in common with Flora Thompson), had in the mid-1980s started a group called 'The Selborne Circle of Rural Writers'. Her intention was to bring together the work of an extraordinary cluster of country and natural history writers, including White, William Cobbett, Richard Jefferies, W. H. Hudson and George Sturt, all of whom had lived in or written of the Hampshire weald and its borderlands, and a growing band of contemporary local historians, naturalists and poets, also in thrall to the area. I was astonished to find a woodcut of my own features on the Circle's notepaper amongst images of the illustrious founding fathers, on the slender grounds that I was writing the biography of one of their number. I was even more surprised to find that I was next to an equally grainy cameo of Flora Thompson.

I must confess, rather shamefacedly, that at this point I hadn't read *Lark Rise to Candleford*. But I knew it was rooted in a very different and distant stretch of countryside, the Oxfordshire arable plain, and assumed that Flora had been rooted there too. Not a bit of it. I was probably the only member of the Circle who did not know that she had spent the thirty years between 1898 (when she was twenty-two) and 1928 in or on the borders of Hampshire. It was here she laboriously, patiently, taught herself the craft of writing, without any help from or contact with the conventional literary world. She began as a contributor of short stories to women's magazines, progressed to become the author of an apparently non-fiction journal (run as a magazine column) about nature and local people. 'The Peverel Papers', as the journal was called, patently echo the work of Gilbert White, who in addition to *The Natural History of Selborne* (a book Thompson doted on) himself composed a daily journal that covers almost four decades. But they also echo, in a different sense, the resonant topography of the Hampshire landscape itself;

and part of the story I have tried to unravel here is why this particular location should have had such an influence on Flora, on White before her, and, it transpired, on me. I have meandered around this area for the past thirty years and can still feel its latent poetry, its physical rhythms, bouncing between the three of us.

The fact of Flora's westward migration (she left 'Lark Rise' aged fourteen and only returned once during the rest of her life) and the nature of what she wrote en route cast a new light on the kind of book *Lark Rise to Candleford* is. It demolishes for a start the myth of Thompson as a kind of 'primitive' or 'naive' author. This is an assumption frequently made about rural writers who weren't embedded in the literary establishment.* We like the idea of the hedge-scribe, whose words pour out as instinctively as birdsong. It helps bolster our myth of the countryside as a refuge from the intellectual affectations of the town. A reading of *Lark Rise* in the light of what Flora had written before, and of the slow and complex evolution of its style and contents, shows that, on the contrary, she was a sophisticated and imaginative writer, involved in a more complicated business than straight-forward autobiography. At the heart of this process, as I shall discuss later, was the creation of 'Laura' (evidently a version of her childhood self) to act as a third-person 'character' in what otherwise seems like a memoir – except that Flora

* For example, the patronizing praise given to the Oxford-educated and highly intellectual Gilbert White. John Burroughs wrote of White that 'the privacy and preoccupation of the author are like those of the bird building her nest, or of the bee gathering her sweets . . .' James Russell Lowell linked White with Izaak Walton (of *Compleat Angler* fame) as a species of naive writers: 'Nature had endowed these men with the simple skill to make happiness out of the cheap material that is within the means of the poorest of us. The good fairy gave them to weave cloth of gold out of straw.'

writes none of it in the first person. So the books have, in a sense, two narrators: the adult Flora reflecting on past events, and her young *Doppelgänger* observing them directly. The counterpoint (and occasional puzzlement) created by these dual viewpoints is part of what gives *Lark Rise* its unique voice.

Flora's evident artistry as a storyteller has also raised worries amongst some critics and historians about authenticity. Put simply, was Flora Thompson 'making things up'? Was she glamorizing the life of poor Oxfordshire rural people for the sake of a good story, and helping to perpetuate the fantasy (still alive in our culture) of a lost rural arcadia? The answer to the first question is almost certainly yes – Flora was an accomplished fiction writer and admits so herself. But it seems to me this is the wrong kind of question. In *Lark Rise*, Flora was never attempting to write either a straight memoir or an objective social history, but something more nuanced, an imaginative reconstruction of what life felt like to a growing country child in those last years of the nineteenth century.

And this frames the real story of Flora's life as a fascinating paradox. Her fame comes from her commemoration of the virtues of traditional village life and people. Yet her own history consisted chiefly of an escape from this culture, and a hunger to become a different kind of person, a writer with her sights on the skies, not rutted in the agricultural vales. The story I have pieced together in the following pages is about how her developing imagination enabled these conflicting affections to coexist – and eventually be reconciled – by writing a tribute to a life from which she had, in effect, emigrated. It is a story of roots, aspiration and escape which still has strong resonances today.

A note on Flora and Laura

When the story is evidently being told retrospectively, by the adult Flora, I narrate it in the past tense. When it is, as it were, delegated to Laura, as an observer or participant in the action, I use the present tense, as if Laura were a character in a novel.

1. Juniper Hill: 'a gentle rise in the flat'

The hamlet stood on a gentle rise in the flat, wheat-growing north-east corner of Oxfordshire. We will call it Lark Rise because of the great number of skylarks which made the surrounding fields their springboard and nested on the bare earth between the rows of green corn . . . To a child it seemed that it must always have been so; but the ploughing and sowing and reaping were recent innovations. Old men could remember when the Rise, covered with juniper bushes, stood in the midst of a furzy heath – common land, which had come under the plough after the passing of the Inclosure Acts.

Lark Rise to Candleford

Flora Thompson's life and work is a story of the relationship between people and place, and the two still refract each other even when her story is told in quite new ways.

In 2010, in the early stages of researching this book, I happened to stay the night in a farmhouse B&B in the folded limestone country near Bath. It was a balmy Saturday evening in September and, taking an amble around the farm, I came across something very curious, marooned in the yard. It had the look of a decrepit settlement, a recently abandoned village, a rural *Mary Celeste*. There were two rows of cottages facing each other, with a dusty track between them. The walls seemed to be made of stucco, not local Bath stone, and were stained with yellow lichen. There were clean curtains in the windows. The gardens were in good order, with sweet peas in flower and rows of fat cabbages. It was a vision of an English village as idyllic as a Helen Allingham painting – except there was not a soul to be seen. I edged round the back of the cottages and realized they were two-dimensional. They had that element much prized by householders, façade, but nothing behind. The walls were shored-up plasterboard, painted with stone-coloured acrylic. The lichens were a clever piece of distressing, applied (with considerable botanical exactitude, I should add) by a paint-spray. And it dawned on me that I was wandering through some kind of reproduction, a simulacrum, though of what I hadn't the slightest idea.

Next morning, the proprietor – the farmer's wife – was happy to explain. It was one of the sets for the television production of *Lark Rise to Candleford*. The BBC had leased the space at the back of the farm for the duration of the series. She was full of admiration for the set-designers, who, she said, had once been hired to conjure up an Arabian Nights fantasy for the wedding party of a rich sheikh. No wonder they had made such a convincing job of a humble Victorian hamlet. To tell the truth, the facsimile looked rather more authentic 'resting' between series in the autumn sunshine than it did blazed yellow by floodlights and hoed free of weeds on the television screen.

The farmer had also leased to the BBC a large field adjacent to the mock village, so that a rough road could be made through the crops, which could in turn be sown and cut according to the filming schedule. The production team had not been so historically smart here, and had omitted to sow the poppies and cornflowers that would have adorned any nineteenth-century wheatfield. But that seemed a minor

environmental anachronism compared to the huge geographical disjunction* involved in moving the action to Wessex.

There were good practical reasons why the production team
chose this site rather than the real (and still extant) settlements
in north Oxfordshire where *Lark Rise* is set. Some kind of semi-
permanent set had to be built. It would have been impossible to
occupy and de-modernize for four years not just an entire village but parts of a nearby market town (a facsimile of this, plus
interiors, had been built in a farm a mile away from the ersatz
Lark Rise). But deciding to base the sets in a quite different landscape from arable Oxfordshire necessarily involved cultural
judgements as well as production practicalities. The countryside around the real twenty-first-century Juniper Hill (the
hamlet on which Lark Rise is modelled) is not visually inviting,
and superficially not at all like the idyllic landscapes of our
pastoral imagination. It's cut across by pylons and telephone
wires and made hazy by the constant drone of road traffic. The
fields are flat and hedgeless, and dominated by intensive arable
farming. There is no woodland, and barely a scrap of accessible
unfarmed green space. The furzy common covered with juniper bushes that gave the original hamlet its name is as lost a
domain as it was at the end of the nineteenth century.

The Avon hills chosen by the BBC are, however uninten-
tionally, much closer to the landscape of the rural dream. They

---

* There is an obsolete word for this topographical equivalent of anachronism,
which should be revived, given how frequently these inappropriate displacements occur in film and literature. The *OED* gives 'anatopism' and a definition
from Thomas de Quincey as a 'geographical blunder'. I rather like the suggestion of my lexicophile friend Robert Macfarlane, who offers 'ectopic', used as
an adjective. This has the advantage of resonances from the field of medicine,
where one meaning describes a missed heartbeat or one occurring in the
'wrong' place. It would also generate the noun 'ectopia', which sounds like a
place one would prefer not to be.

have grand vistas, rich pastures, and woods big enough for pheasants and poachers. They have a multitude of green hideaways and look-outs, spots where characters can sit under the trees and chat. Through the camera lens they presented a benign setting which seemed perennially fertile both for the growing of crops and the nurturing of close and neighbourly relations.

The industrial agriculture of Juniper Hill today offers no such topographical freedoms. It was not much better when Flora was living there. There was no remaining common land, and the villagers worked on low wages on other men's acres. The essential identity of 'Lark Rise' – the mutually supportive, inward-looking community, the wagon-circle of subsistence – was in part a reaction against a niggardly, ungenerous environment, not a product of abundance and availability. In one sense, the television set was a mirage, allowing the stories to be played out in the arcadia of our national imagination, not in the kind of landscape where they would have carried more conviction. But it provided a salutary lesson in cultural preconceptions, and I for one had been briefly fooled into thinking I was in an authentic relic of the Victorian countryside. Was the fabricated hamlet a replica of what was already a fake? Had Flora Thompson been as adept with her paint-spray as the designer, creating an artful, two-dimensional deception that has continually bewitched us because it is what we expect – what we *need* – to keep our dreams alive?

There is now just a single juniper bush growing in Juniper Hill. It crouches in the front garden of a private house that until the 1990s was still the hamlet's pub, the Fox Inn. Before that it was part of a colony of the shrubs, unusual or extensive enough to lend their name to the settlement that grew up around them.

The first page of *Lark Rise* describes how a 'Rise, covered with juniper bushes, stood in the midst of a furzy heath', and a contemporary local historian, J. C. Blomfield, confirms this. 'On some ground [close-by], the low evergreen bushy shrub, known as the Common Juniper, grew in abundance. Its hard wood was useful fuel, and its spicy berries may have been beneficial as medicines. Hence this spot came to be known in recent times as Juniper Hill.'

Blomfield sidesteps the shrub's medicinal potency. It had a long-standing reputation as an abortifacient, and up until the mid-1990s juniper pills were still being advertised as 'The Ladies' Friend' in women's magazines. But it wasn't juniper's handy pharmacological properties that led to the settlement being established amongst the bushes. Juniper is a species that in southern England is almost exclusively confined to chalky soils. What the shrubs indicated, growing conspicuously on a swell of ground in an otherwise unpromisingly infertile waste, was a patch of mineral-rich, well-drained soil. They were a signal as clear as palm trees in a desert: here was a good spot for a garden and a house, and maybe a few wells. The settlement of Juniper Hill wasn't just named for its juniper bushes; it sprang from the same basic resource as they did.

That Flora Thompson spent her childhood in this comparatively fertile corner of what had once been pure heathland, is among the more important circumstantial influences on her life and work. That it was no longer a common was as significant as the fact that it once had been, and within living memory. The inhabitants of Juniper Hill during Flora's time there remembered the folk-ways of the people who had once used the area as common land (for grazing cattle and gathering fuel, for example). But most common rights were extinguished by the enclosure of the heath in 1869, as was the physical heath itself. And by the 1880s, when Flora was a child, the old privileges were chiefly rehearsed as shadow-play, rituals of memory, or small hobbyist contributions to the domestic economy. In the main, the villagers were experiencing the rigours of uncertain, wage-dependent labour in the middle of a serious agricultural depression, and that lent the details of their lives a different kind of urgency. The tensions between 'old romance' and the challenges of modernization, and between fatalism and mutual help, are what give *Lark Rise* its energy as a story. They may also have been part of the reason Flora Thompson got out of the area as fast and as unrepentantly as she did.

The cottage in which Flora lived for the first fifteen years of her life was on the southern edge of the hamlet, and was called – providentially, for someone whose life was destined to be lived on the margins – 'The End House'. It's still possible to stand at the bottom of what would have been her garden and gaze out over an arable fieldscape looking much as it must have done in her day – except that in the distance now, on the far side of the Oxford road, are the futuristic domes and masts of the Croughton wireless station, the modern descendant of the telegraph machines Flora would one day operate in her work as a Post Office assistant.

But back in the mid eighteenth century this view would still have been over an uninterrupted expanse of heather and furze, and it was in this landscape that the first shoots of Juniper Hill arose. 'Cotsford Heath' is marked on a 1797 map as an area of rough common land north-west of the village of Cotsford (known as Cottisford today, and fictionalized as 'Fordlow' in *Lark Rise*). The heath was used by the villagers for grazing, gathering gorse and juniper for fuel, and foraging for herbs and flowers for food and medicine. The hamlet had its origins in two 'poor's houses' built in 1754 by the overseers of the poor, who later added two more cottages.

Flora's account is more glamorized. She has the foundations of the hamlet, semi-fictionalized as 'Lark Rise', laid by six free-holders, who built their own houses using materials close at hand in a way that had been used for vernacular buildings for hundreds of years. 'The walls were of furze branches closely pressed together and daubed with a mixture of mud and mor-tar,' and later they were improved, given thatched roofs, coats of whitewash and diamond-paned windows. Flora may have been ignorant of the true beginnings of the hamlet, but could equally well have been rounding off the facts to suit the image of the community she wanted to present. But her description fits the creation of the second wave of dwellings in Juniper Hill. Over the next fifty years, more than thirty houses – all, save four, unauthorized self-builds by squatters on the open common – were established in the hamlet.

This did not go down well with the gentry. The enclosure of common land by parliamentary enactment was in full swing at this time, and in 1847, the local landowners, Eton College and the Tusmore Park estate (just south of Juniper Hill), made a formal application to enclose the heath and convert it into pri-vate agricultural land. The response by the people of Juniper Hill was prompt and physical. They tore down the enclosure notices from Cottisford church door. They drove the surveyors off the common and dumped their tape measures and theodo-lites in the scrub. Later they dealt out similar rough justice to two magistrates and a constable who had come to try and enforce the survey. The authorities responded by issuing threats to the squatters, alluding sinisterly to the parallel 'Irish' troubles, and doubtless remembering the much more serious violence that had occurred during the enclosure of Otmoor, just ten miles away.* The hamlet resisted for six years, during which time what was called the Juniper Hill 'Mob' would not allow even a spade to be dug into the heath. But eventually the landowners' patience ran out and they instituted proceedings at court. Some of the squatters reluctantly settled. In August 1853, a gang of twenty hired mercenaries, armed with pick-axes, threatened to demolish the homes of the remainder, forcing them to compromise too. The deal was that they could harvest their crops that summer, and have fourteen-year leases of their cottages. After that term the properties would revert to the landowners.

.

And so Juniper Hill metamorphosed into a curious kind of post-enclosure village. The cottages were leased out by the Tusmore Park estate and Eton College (though the latter seems not to have insisted on the agreed reversion after fourteen years). The male farm-workers became wage-labourers, chiefly at Manor Farm, Cottisford, and were no longer able to supplement their earnings from the beneficence of the heath. The land was ploughed, divided up into individual fields, and lost many of its ancient pathways. One of these fields is figured on an 1898 sale plan in the Bodleian Library and has the name of

* The resistance against the enclosure of Otmoor (successfully petitioned for by the Duke of Marlborough) was one of the most heroic in the nine-teenth century. In 1829 more than a thousand people marched around the seven-mile boundary of the moor, tearing down all the fences. The Yeo-manry arrived and the Riot Act was read, but the commoners refused to disperse. Forty-four were arrested and sent off in the direction of Oxford gaol. But it was the day of Oxford's St Giles' Fair, and a great crowd of sym-pathizers ambushed the troop convoy and released the prisoners. The commoners fought on for another ten years, but the enclosure was eventu-ally imposed by superior force. Today, happily, much of it has been 'unenclosed' and is a thriving wetland nature reserve.

'Lark Rise', and just to its north-west is the squarish block marking the house where Flora Thompson, then Flora Timms, spent her childhood.

2.   Flora Timms: the awkward daughter

Flora Timms was actually born not in 'The End House' but ('for convenience', she writes cryptically) in another, and probably rougher, dwelling in the hamlet, which belonged to her mother's older sister, Harriet. The house (later demolished) was called, mysteriously, Watford Tunnel Cottage, and in *Lark Rise* – Laura perhaps being the implicit narrator of this important moment in her life – the day of her birth, 5 December 1876, is described dramatically as one of deep snow, though weather records show it was a normal early winter's day of showers and gusty winds. Flora was weaving romance around her life from its very inception.

Her parents, Albert and Emma Timms, had been married in July the previous year and they made a complementary pair, an underachieving but idealistic husband balanced by a business-like but imaginative wife. Albert Timms was a jobbing builder who had come from a family of stonemasons. His father, Thomas, had worked in Bicester, close to Juniper Hill, and Albert was born in 1854 in the market town of Buckingham, the chief model for Candleford in the *Lark Rise* books. Albert took up the family trade directly after leaving school, and as a precociously talented carver in the early 1870s, he went to work on the restoration of the ceiling of Bath Abbey, where the crumbling lath and plaster was being replaced with stone fan-tracery. He must have felt like an early astronaut freed from the earthly tethers of his fellow workers. 'They used to haul him to places inaccessible from a ladder or scaffolding,' Flora remembers his mother saying, 'in a cage-like arrangement at the end of a long rope. My mother [-in-law] dreaded to go near the place, lest she should see him dangling like a gigantic spider in space.'

When Albert came down to earth and to more humble work in Oxfordshire in his late teens, he was already more worldly than most of his friends and neighbours. He'd become an agnostic and a socialist. He'd also developed a sense of embitterment quite at odds with his years. A legend that the Timms family had fallen from grace, that they were once part of a bejewelled branch of the Oxfordshire Wallingtons,* melded corrosively with Albert's thwarted dreams of becoming a sculptor. Instead he had to settle for humdrum repair work on local churches and chipping out a few fragments of home-grown statuary – a child's head, a stone lion. Drink became an early – and regular – consolation.

But so did Emma Dibber, whom he met at one of the churches where he was working. Emma was born in 1853 in the village of Ardley, a few miles south of Juniper Hill, in a cottage next to the churchyard. Her parents, John and Hannah, were both from local families and her father followed the trade of 'eggler', collecting eggs from local farms and smallholdings in a pony and cart and selling them in nearby market towns. But his more creative leisure enthusiasms proved a deeper influence on his daughter and, by family osmosis perhaps, on Flora too. Ardley church had a small musician's gallery, similar to the one in Mellstock church in Thomas Hardy's *Under the*

---

* The myth of a high-born ancestry, and possibly a lost fortune to go with it, wasn't uncommon in poor rural families, sometimes as a piece of morale-boosting fantasy when times were hard, sometimes based on a fragment of real historical evidence. It's part of the dramatic basis of Thomas Hardy's *Tess of the d'Urbervilles*, for example. In the Timmses' case, Flora had vague childhood memories of seeing faded daguerreotypes of ladies in crinolines, resplendent in gold bracelets.

Greenwood Tree. John Dibber played the violin in the Ardley church band. In *Lark Rise*, Flora tells how this love of music – and much else – was passed on to her mother. The rector of Ardley lived with his more aged sister, a Miss Lowe, who had become fond of the 'pretty, fair-haired little girl at the church-yard cottage ... Little Emma [Flora, unusually, uses her mother's real Christian name in the books] had a sweet voice and she was supposed to go there for singing lessons; but she had learned other things, too, including old-world manners and to write a beautiful antique hand with delicate, open-looped pointed letters and long "s's", such as her instructress and other young ladies had been taught in the last quarter of the eighteenth century.'

As was the custom at the time, Emma Dibber went into ser-vice at the age of twelve, but her parents were sensitive to the fact she was culturally a cut above her peers, and with the help of the Revd Lowe, found her a position in the nearby hamlet of Fewcott, where the curate Henry Jocelyne and his wife Mary needed a nursemaid for their expanding family. Flora suggests that Emma developed a skill for storytelling there, helped by the fact that the eldest Jocelyne child, Louise Elizabeth, was much the same age as her, and it was a gift that she was to use to lasting effect with her own children.

So Flora grew up with two far from retiring parents, with different but complementary temperaments. In *Lark Rise* she writes of her mother with admiration, for her imagination and frugality and independence. About her father, she is more ambivalent. She respected his moments of strength and individuality of mind, but was well aware of his resent-ments and drinking habits. While Flora and her younger brother Edwin (born in 1879) were growing up, Albert

Timms worked chiefly for a builder in Brackley, putting up cottages, repairing walls, helping with extensions to the gentry's houses. Just occasionally he was able to put his mason's skills to use in carving names on tombstones, but spending much of his life at mundane building work frustrated him, and Flora portrays him as a difficult father and husband. His erratic progress at work – doubtless matched by erratic moods – is traced out on the birth certificates of his children in Cottisford church. At Flora's birth in 1876, he is listed as a labourer/mason; for the next seven children as a labourer; the next two as a mason; and for the final child in 1898 down to a bricklayer again. Throughout this period he is one of the few male residents of Juniper Hill who does not work as an agricultural labourer. The census of 1881 records five such, including the innkeeper and a retired farm bailiff. Albert's oddity of occupation, frequent absences from the hamlet and uncompromising political views made him something of a misfit locally.

Having parents who, in their different ways, were both on the margins of hamlet society may have contributed to the slight sense of exclusion Flora complains of throughout her early life, of being an analytical observer of village society more than an unselfconscious participant. ('Laura Looks On' is the title given to one of the chapters in *Over to Candleford*, the second part of *Lark Rise to Candleford*.) She was an introspective child and had difficulties empathizing with her peers, something she compensated for by an acute attention to the surface details of people and things. The almost filmic beginning of *Lark Rise* – 'The hamlet stood on a gentle rise in the flat, wheat-growing north-east corner of Oxfordshire' – in which the narrator's viewpoint gently spirals in from a high prospect of the surrounding landscape, pans across the scatter of cottages, and finally zooms in on 'one house . . . a little apart, and turning its back on its neighbours, as though about to run away into the fields', is a clever, retrospectively constructed introduction to the author's home, not at all a child's memory. But when, a few chapters later, young Laura is given the opportunity to describe the hamlet, she also ponders it from afar, with a convincingly childlike twist: 'To Laura, as a child, the hamlet once appeared as a fortress. She was coming home alone from school one wild, grey, March afternoon, and, looking up from her battling against the wind, got a swift new impression of the cluster of stark walls and slated roofs on the Rise, with rooks tumbling and clouds hurrying overhead, smoke beating down from the chimneys, and clothes on clothes-lines straining away in the wind. "It's a fort! It's a fort!" she cried, and she went on up the road, singing in her flat, tuneless little voice the Salvation Army hymn of the day, "Hold the fort, for I am coming."'

The concept of the hamlet as a metaphorical fortress, a tight-knit community under siege by the modern world, is one that surfaces often in *Lark Rise* – though not as strikingly as the sense of it as a *reservation*, in which Flora (and Laura) gazes about like an indigenous anthropologist, missing nothing, but always slightly on the outside of things. She observes the hamlet goings-on without judgement and, in John Fowles's word, as an extraordinary 'remembrancer'.

She puts on record vivid accounts of great rural set-pieces, like the May Queen rituals. But – her crucial accounts of the domestic life of the hamlet women apart, as we shall see – her accounts of rural work are chiefly agricultural. Almost every able-bodied man in the hamlet (Flora's father being a conspicuous exception) worked on the land. Her stories of the annual killing of the house-pig remain the definitive accounts of this imperative ritual and catch its emotional ambivalence every bit as well as its bloody detail. But there are smaller vignettes of farming life, too, whose precise and intimate detailing is more revealing, and carries greater conviction, than any literary equivalent of landscape painting could. For example, at lunchtime, the more fortunate of the 'Men Afield' 'had bread and cold bacon, perhaps the top or the bottom of a cottage loaf, on which the small cube of bacon was placed, with a finger of bread on top, called the thumb-piece, to keep the meat untouched by hand and in position for manipulation with a clasp-knife. The consumption of this food was managed neatly and decently, a small sliver of bacon and a chunk of bread being cut and conveyed to the mouth in one movement.' The women who still worked in the fields also had their own etiquette. They never worked in the same field as the men, but elsewhere, at their own special, often rougher or more menial tasks: stone-picking, weeding, mending sacks in the barn in wet weather. *Lark Rise* contains what is probably the last account of the ancient and disappearing practice of gleaning, or 'leazing' as it was called locally, in which the hamlet women and children 'swarmed over the stubble' after harvest, gathering the wheat-ears the horse-rake had missed, to be ground into flour for their daily puddings. 'Up and down and over and over the stubble they hurried, backs bent, eyes on the ground, one hand outstretched to pick up the ears, the other resting on the small of the back with the "handful".' This is the precise position of one of the women in Millet's painting *The Gleaners*, made in northern France in 1857, an extraordinary testament to the often universal forms of vernacular customs.

But the bulk of Flora's documentary writing in *Lark Rise* concerns the non-agricultural, domestic life in the hamlet, and the characters that live it out. There is always the possibility that she is fictionalizing some of this material, but it has a persuasive sense of detail, of 'inside knowledge' that makes you trust her. We're told about ancestral children's games and the young men's bawdy storytelling. We're introduced to the improvised fanciness – unknown in previous generations of the rural working class – with which the younger wives were beginning to adorn their cottages: gridirons covered with pink wool and tinsel and hung up to serve as letter racks; a plethora of bows – on cushion covers, on photograph frames, even on the handle of the pot under the bed. The women's ingenuity at thrift was boundless. The younger ones shared their clothes. Two especially poor women, Bessie and her mother (who sat all day at the window earning a pittance from lace-making), even shared their smidgen of bacon. 'It was said that when the two women fried a rasher for their midday meal . . . they took it in turn to have the rasher, the other one dipping her bread in the fat, day and day about.' They produced a favourite alternative to butter (then, at tenpence a pound, too extravagant for general use) by blending rosemary leaves with lard. If the women had responsibility for their herb patches, the men, once they'd finished work in the fields, looked after the vegetables (and sometimes small patches of corn) in the small allotment gardens they'd been granted in exchange for the loss of their common rights. Echoes of the old culture of collective improvisation reverberated even in these minimal remnants.

Some of the women Flora introduces were formidable inheritors of the arts of making do. 'Old Sally', one of the oldest inhabitants of Lark Rise, who claimed to have inherited one of the original squatters' cottages (it was in fact owned by her downtrodden husband, Dick), was an active villager, and would have been an eager contributor to the weekend WI stall, had such a thing yet existed. She brewed her own beer, grew a collection of old-fashioned roses that would have done credit to a mansion garden, and curated the hamlet's time of day. Her large and loud grandfather clock told not just the hour but the day of the week and the changes of the moon. 'The clock portion kept such good time that half the hamlet set its own clocks by it. The other half preferred to follow the hooter at the brewery in the market town, which could be heard when the wind was in the right quarter. So there were two times in the hamlet and people would say when asking the hour, "Is that hooter time, or Old Sally's?"'

The best known of all Flora's female characters is Queenie Macey, hamlet earth-mother, keeper of the gossip, brewer of herbal nostrums, a figure who is both comic and mystical. Flora's vivid portrait of the woman who lived in the tiny one-up one-down cottage next to the End House runs to not much more than 2,000 words, but succeeds in knitting together an acute sketch of Queenie's personality with a real sense of the changes both she and rural society were experiencing at this critical moment in their history. (Flora had had some practice at perfecting this blend of biography and cultural tone-poem, since a journalistic sketch of Queenie in 1936 would be the first step in the evolution of *Lark Rise*.) Flora paints Queenie as a survivor of an earlier generation of hamlet-dwellers, who grew up before enclosure in the 1850s.

Juniper Hill was more prosperous at that time, and some of the women made moderate livings as lace-makers. Half a century later, in *Lark Rise*, Queenie, last of their kind, sits outside her cottage demonstrating her arcane skills to an enthralled audience, like one of those living manikins in modern heritage exhibitions. In this case the lookers-on are the hamlet children, who watch her conjuring lace bobbins as if they are ornaments on a secular rosary. 'They loved to see the bobbins tossed hither and thither . . . every bobbin weighted with its bunch of bright beads and every bunch with its own story, which they had heard so many times that they knew it by heart, how this bunch had been part of a blue bead necklace worn by her little sister who had died at five years old, and this other one had belonged to her mother, and that black one had been found, after she was dead, in a work-box belonging to a woman who was reputed to have been a witch.' Queenie is also an apiarist, not just a bee-keeper but a bee-whisperer. Her bees have to be communicated with, to be told when there has been a death in the household, or 'tanged' more loudly by the beating of a spoon on a shovel if the swarm has strayed outside her territory.

Queenie's husband Tom, better known as Twister, is 'a small, thin-legged, jackdaw-eyed old fellow', with a taste for eccentric clothes that included a gamekeeper's velveteen coat and a bowler hat with a peacock's feather stuck in it. But Flora portrays him as very much the one in the marriage who does *not* wear the trousers. Twister is kind-hearted but feckless, and grabs any chance, legal or otherwise, of earning a shilling, but is more likely to spend it on drink than anything useful for his family. One night, very drunk, he beats Queenie with his belt. The next evening, she lays a pie on his plate, baked golden-brown and decorated with a pastry tulip: 'such a pie as must have seemed to him to illustrate the old saying: "*A woman, a dog and a walnut tree, the more you beat 'em the better they be*"'. When Tom cuts it open, 'curled up inside, was the leather strap with which he had beaten his wife'. He never laid a finger on her again.

Twister contracted pneumonia, so Flora relates, after valiantly trying to rescue a young boy thought to have been buried in 'the great snowstorm', probably of 1890.* Flora passes on her own – or the hamlet's – legend of Twister's surprising burst of selflessness. 'They said he worked then as he had never worked before in his life; his strength and energy were marvellous.' The story has Twister dying of his illness within a fortnight.

Flora's characters are colourful and romantic, but never senti-mentalized. They lose their livelihoods, suffer, sometimes die in poverty, or in foreign wars. But there are enough discrepan-cies between her accounts of their lives and the documentary evidence that exists about the real people they are evidently modelled on to raise questions about the kind of stories Flora was telling. Sally and Dick are identifiable from the 1881 census as Sarah and Richard Moss. But Sally's grandfather was not one of the original squatters, as Flora (or Sally herself) contends, nor was it his house that she moved into on her marriage. The Mosses came from Northamptonshire. Sarah was born at Helmsdon in 1812 and only moved to Cottisford Heath after marrying George Fox, who had built a squatter's cottage there in 1847. She did not marry Richard Moss until 1869, after their first respective partners had died, so Flora's suggestion of a sixty-year marriage isn't accurate.

Queenie Macey, as portrayed by Flora, has probably absorbed some of Sarah Moss's characteristics. But she seems chiefly based on Eliza Massey, née Gee, born in Fringford in 1841. Eliza married Thomas Massey in 1850, and in the 1851 census they

---

* The snowfalls of 1890–91, which lasted from 25 November 1890 until 22 January 1891, were the most severe winter weather to occur during Flora Thompson's time in Juniper Hill. The Thames was frozen for over a mile near Twickenham, and the River Dee near Chester for five and a half miles.

were living in Launton, ten miles south of Juniper Hill. They moved to the hamlet sometime in the late 1850s. By this time lace-making as a cottage industry had been all but wiped out by the invention of the Nottingham mechanical lace-maker, and the skills Queenie showed off to the local children were being practised on a purely leisure basis. In the 1861 census, lace-making is not listed as the main occupation of any woman. Thomas 'Twister' Massey died in Bicester Union Workhouse in 1899 aged seventy, and a long time after his supposed hero-ism in the great blizzard. After his death, Queenie lived on parish relief and the support of her friends and children. She survived until 1902, when she too died in Bicester, at her daugh-ter's house.

★

When they were small, 'Laura' and her brother 'Edmund' (Flora's real-life brother Edwin was born in 1878) were often taken for a walk by their mother along the turnpike road to the west of the hamlet, and would never pass the milestone until its inscription had been read out to them: 'OXFORD XIX MILES'. The concept of this distant city nagged at them, and they pestered adults with questions about it. Their mother said it was called a city because a bishop lived there and it held an annual fair, but that was all she knew. Another said the wages could be 25 shillings a week but you'd spend half that on rent, and there was nowhere to keep a pig. They might have learned more if they'd asked their father Albert, who had lived there as a child, when his parents had kept a public house in the city. But he was sensitive about his past, and talk about it was apt to bring on fits of irritable resent-ment about his supposed 'fall'. None of the other villagers would have thought the presence of a great university in the city either significant or remotely relevant.

Education in Lark Rise meant seven or eight years at the National School at Fordlow (modelled on Cottisford, a mile south-east of Juniper Hill). Laura began there at the age of six, with a head-start as reader as a result of being taught by her father, with the help of *Mavor's First Reader*. It was a conventional village school, with the curriculum heavily influenced by the Church. Laura confesses that she was useless at maths and needlework, but precocious at reading and writing. The Fordlow teacher, Miss Holmes (Miss Holmyard in reality) taught her to write, and by the time she was seven she was penning competent verse and home-grown journalism. In a memoir entitled 'A Country Child Taking Notes', published in 1947, Flora recalls: 'I never could remember in after-life when I began to write, but at seven years old I was penning letters in rhyme to Santa Claus, to be attached to my own and my brother's Christmas stockings, and a little later, I was running a family magazine, which continued until my mother's grocer changed the colour of his sugar wrapping-paper from greyish-white to a very dark blue, upon which no ink would show, and so caused me to experience my first paper shortage.' Flora may be glamorizing the extent of her childhood literacy, but her name can be seen in the Diocesan Inspector's report on Cottisford School for 7 June 1888, when she won the annual Diocesan Prize for an essay on the life of Moses.

Laura's real education was out in the lanes and fields, and listening to her mother's stories at home. All the Lark Rise children walked to school, along a mile and a half of lanes, carrying hot potatoes to eat at lunchtime and 'to warm their hands on the way', and scrumping turnips, young peas and wheat-ears from the adjoining fields. It was a riotous procession of foraging, marble-playing, bird's-nesting, brawling farm kids, and Laura was often nervous in their company. Once Edmund had started school and she had a companion, Laura would take him on the cross-country route instead (at least in dry weather), a far more exciting track, still navigable today, that went through a small covert called Cuckoo Clump and past the lakes and ornamental shrubberies of Cottisford House.

It's on these outdoor explorations that Laura's rapt attention to (and Flora's recall of) the intricate, physical detail of the world becomes so evident. She is enthralled by the exotic contents of the street-trader Jerry's cart: oranges, with their 'strange foreign scent', and pith which could be dried on the hob and taken to school as a kind of chewing gum; the 'cool colours and queer shapes' of the fish which Laura imagined swimming through seaweed, especially John Dories, with their black eye-spot, which Jerry explained as being the thumbprint of St Peter, the patron saint of fishermen. Laura details the precise atmosphere of late summer mornings when the harvest was imminent; the hamlet up and about before dawn, the smell of bacon and wood fires overpowering the earthy, early morning scent of the fields. And mushrooming, done sometimes against her parents' wishes because the wet pastures meant 'Six shillingsworth of good shoe-leather gone for sixpen'orth of mushrooms!' But some years a pair of old boots was kept expressly for this purpose, and this exactly located detail – the mother's generosity, the boots kept downstairs so that walking out in them wouldn't disturb the younger children's sleep – is as sharply evocative as the memory of Laura and Edmund's feet leaving 'long, dark trails on the dewy turf'.

Flora was especially sensitive to smell. She recalls the aroma of Old Sally's 'kitchen-storeroom' with the analytic discrimination of a wine-taster: 'The apple crop was stored on racks suspended beneath the ceiling and bunches of herbs dangled below. In one corner stood the big brewing copper in which Sally still brewed with good malt and hops once a quarter. The scent of the last brewing hung over the place till the next and mingled with the apple and onion and dried thyme and sage smells, with a dash of soapsuds thrown in, to compound the aroma which remained in the children's memories for life and caused a whiff of any two of the component parts in any part of the world to be recognized with an appreciative sniff and a mental ejaculation of "Old Sally's!".'

The naturalist William Hudson wrote an essay in 1918 about what he called the 'animism' of children.* 'By animism I do not mean the theory of a soul in nature,' he explained, 'but the tendency or impulse or instinct, in which all myth originates, to *animate* all things; the projection of ourselves into nature; the sense and apprehension of an intelligence like our own but more powerful in all visible things. It persists and lives in many of us, I imagine, more than we like to think, or more than we know, especially in those born and bred amidst rural surroundings . . . these being the conditions which are most favourable to it – the scenes which have "inherited associa-tions" for us, as Herbert Spencer has said.'

Hudson reckons he was about eight years old (much the same age as Flora at her most sensually alert) when the raw intensity of his registration of colour, scent and sound, of taste

* Included in his memoir *Far Away and Long Ago* (1918). In the first decades of the twentieth century W. H. Hudson travelled widely in the parts of Hampshire and Surrey that Flora lived in and wrote about later in her life. It's unlikely the two ever met (Flora would have hidden in a bush at the sight of such an inquisitive man about the same business as her). But he was a popular nature writer and ardent conservationist, and it's almost certain that Thompson had read at least some of his work.

and touch – 'the sparkle of sunlight on water, the taste of milk, of fruit, of honey, the smell of dry or moist soil, of wind and rain, of herbs and flowers; the mere feel of a blade of grass' – began to take on a sense of immanent meaning or significance, as if these objects and phenomena contained some impalpable essence beyond their physical reality. They became talismans and totems, sometimes even slightly magical. Flora talks of Queenie's lace bobbins as if they were memory beads. Laura is the first person in the hamlet to experience the exotic taste of tomatoes, the 'love-apples'. And she develops a particular attachment to a bottle of sea-water (she was not to see the real ocean until she was twenty-one). One of the hamlet girls in service at Brighton had brought a medicine bottle of the liquid home as a curiosity. In time it became the property of a younger sister, a classmate of Laura's, who was persuaded to swap it for a slice of cake and a blue-bead necklace. 'Laura treasured it for years', by which time it was doubtless murky and malodorous, a bottleful of nothing but memories and hopes.

*

One summer morning Laura, aged eleven, and her brother Edmund, nine, make the metaphorical journey between Lark Rise and Candleford, between hamlet and town, for real, on foot. It is a rite of passage, their first big expedition without adult escort, and they are dressed for the part, Laura already demonstrating the compulsive fascination with dressing-up that was to continue throughout her life. She is in a green smock, her brother in an 'ex-Sunday' white sailor suit, and both are sporting fashionable 'Zulu hats', plaited out of rushes. As they step out on their eight-mile odyssey, every experience seems, like their clothes, to be an intricate weave of symbol

and sensual detail. Bright colours, sharp allusions, wry memories and dreams of things to come click together like
knitting-needles. The children are intoxicated by their new
freedom and register everything: the mist still rising from the
stooks, and the gleaning women busy in the stubble; the
gathering swallows – already, Laura notes, perfectly familiar
with telegraph wires; the unfamiliar wagons and farmers met
on the road. Asked where they are off to by the wagoners,
Edmund responds 'We are going to Candleford'; they are told,
'Keep puttin' one foot in front o' t'other an' you'll be there
before dark.'

When they do reach the outskirts of the town, 'they saw
what must have looked like a girls' school out for a walk advancing between the hedgerows to meet them'. It is a relief party,
consisting of their cousins and their schoolfriends, bearing tea.
These sophisticated girls initiate Laura into boy-talk, but she is
more taken with the material wonders of the town, the wax
dummies in the drapers' shop, the fishmonger's where 'a whole
salmon reposed on a bed of green reeds with ice sprinkled over
(ice in August! They would never believe it at home).'

Flora always maintained that the county town of Buckingham, eight miles east of Juniper Hill, was her model for
Candleford, but admits that traces of other market towns with
which she was familiar – Brackley, Bicester and Banbury in particular, and maybe others from her later life in Surrey and
Hampshire – found their way into her stories. Buckingham
certainly had a good quota of aunts, uncles and cousins on her
father's side. But the 'Candleford' that Laura and Edmund
visit on that special summer's day, and frequently throughout
their childhood, is modelled much more on the small (real)
town of Twyford, which lies about eight miles south-east of
Juniper Hill. This is where Flora's real 'Uncle Tom' and his

family had his house and business, and where 'Laura' is initiated into the magic of books. This switching between, and merging of, identifiably real places and people, and semi-fictionalized towns and characters (Laura especially), runs through all the books, and reinforces the need to read them as reality-based novels.

Tom was Thomas Whiting, husband of Albert Timms' sister, Ann. He worked as a moderately successful shoemaker in Twyford, and in 1888 had four daughters aged between five and twelve, which accounts for tidal wave of girlhood that greeted Laura and Edmund as they approached the outskirts of the town. Ann doted on her niece and nephew, and gave them more freedom to play and explore than their own mother did. But Tom provided the intellectual spark. His workshop was a kind of salon for the young working-men of the district, who sat around on upturned boxes, smoking and playing dominoes and talking politics. Laura hung about the workshop, eavesdropping. She was expected to leave when the evening sessions began, but if a caller arrived in the day, she sat it out in a corner, under cover of reading a book.

Flora, intent on building up a convincing picture of the origins of her young *Doppelgänger*'s taste for literature, makes a signature piece out of Laura's discovery of Tom's bookishness. The last day of their holiday in 1888 is wet, and the Whiting cousins suggest that they should all go and play in the attic. The attic is full of old, discarded things, especially clothes, and the children spend the morning dressing up for charades, 'an amusement Laura had not heard of before', even though she seems to have spent much of her young life playing it. She finds it entrancing, and, dressed in an apron and shawl, 'the point of the latter trailing on the ground behind her', does a pitch-perfect imitation of Old Queenie, down to the 'Lawks-a-mussy!'

with which she begins most of her speeches. She follows it up with an impersonation of a bride, draped in an old lace curtain and carrying a feather duster for a bouquet. When the rest of the children have disappeared downstairs, Laura contemplates her ragamuffin gown in a tall, cracked mirror. 'But her own reflection did not hold her more than a moment, for she saw in the glass a recess she had not noticed before packed with books. Books on shelves, books in piles on the floor, and still other books in heaps, higgledy-piggledy, as though they had been turned out of sacks. Which they had, no doubt, for she was told afterwards that the collection was the unsaleable remains of a library from one of the large houses in the district.'

Laura loses herself in this pile of literary detritus – a retreat among the leaves of old sermons, lexicons, 'old novels', a 'natural history of the world which might have detained her had there not been so many other vistas to explore', until the cousins come up to call her to dinner. Amy Whiting surprises her deep in Richardson's *Pamela, or Virtue Rewarded* and sings out to her sisters, 'Laura's a bookworm, a bookworm, a bookworm!' But she brings the book down to the dinner table, and asks her mother Ann if Laura might keep it. Ann is doubtful, understanding that it is a love story but not, Flora adds, 'the full extent of its unsuitability for a reader of such tender age'. But Tom encourages her, arguing that 'No book's too old for anybody who is able to enjoy it, and none too young, either.' Asking her to read to him later, while he works, he spares her *Pilgrim's Progress* and the dreaded Slough of Despond, and introduces her instead to Elizabeth Gaskell's *Cranford*, and Laura spends the afternoon in raptures, reading out loud its tales of a rather superior breed of rural women.

Thereafter they make a reading pact. Whenever Laura visited Candleford, and her cousins could be persuaded to go out by themselves, 'she would tap at the door of her uncle's workshop and hear the familiar challenge, "Who goes there?" and reply "Bookworms, Limited".' Tom's reading seminars may have been unofficial but they were rigorous. As well as introducing Laura to new books, he coached her oral skills, correcting her pronunciation and checking her speed and tendency to histrionic expression.

Back home in the End House, there was more opportunistic reading and listening to stories. Laura finds a 'battered old copy' of Belzoni's *Travels** propping open a neighbour's pantry window. She almost certainly browsed the improving parables in the Religious Tract Society's publication, *The Girl's Own Paper*. But she loves her mother's romantic inventions far more. Emma Timms was an artful and inexhaustible teller of tales. The stories that most captivated Laura and her siblings were those that told of secret hideaways and great adventures. 'One story remained with Laura long after hundreds of others had become a blur of pleasurable memory . . . It was about a little girl who crept under a bush on a heath . . . and found a concealed opening which led to an underground palace in which all the furniture and hangings were pale blue and silver . . . The heroine had marvellous adventures, but they left no impression on Laura's mind, while the blue and silver, deep down under the earth, shone with a kind of moonlight radiance in her imagination.' Others approached the status of family legend, especially the legend that the Timmses had high-born ancestors and were once fabulously wealthy. Their favourite was 'Granny's Golden

* Flora would have revelled in Belzoni's picaresque life. Born in Italy, he fled to England and became a circus performer (he was 6ft 7ins tall and a strongman), then went to Egypt as an explorer and self-taught archaeologist. His account of his adventures was published in 1820.

Footstool'. It told how their paternal grandfather, 'either going to, or coming from' the inn he owned in Oxford, had helped their grandmother into a carriage and placed a box containing a thousand pounds in gold at her feet, saying 'It's not every lady who can ride in her own carriage with a golden footstool.' The story ended abruptly there, too close for comfort to her father's grievances about 'coming down in the world'; and the children were left to fantasize about where the gold might have gone and what they would do with it if it ever came back into the family's possession. Flora was exposed early to the nagging power of neediness and aspiration.

When she left school aged fourteen, Flora was probably no more moody than any other teenager. But the obsession with reading and the introspective fugues that she attributes to her young fictional self begin to annoy her mother (somewhat unfairly, since it had been Emma who had encouraged Flora's taste for stories in the first place). The time was approaching fast when Laura would have to earn her own living and Emma worried what possible future there could be for her impractical misfit of a daughter. Perhaps a nursemaid was the only answer. But there is a showdown one day when Laura is nursing the Timmses' latest baby, 'with a book in her hand and, absent-mindedly, put down the little hand which was trying to clutch her long hair'. Her mother is furious. 'Laura, I'm sorry to say it, but I'm downright disappointed in you . . . I've been watching you for the last ten minutes with that little innocent on your lap and your head stuck in that nasty old book and not so much as one look at his pretty ways. (Didums, didums neglect him then, the little precious! Anybody who could read a book with you on their lap must have a heart of stone . . .) No, it won't do, Laura. You'll never make a nurse, sorry as I am to say so.'

So Emma abandons her hope that Laura might join the annual diaspora of village girls in the role of a nursemaid. Laura understandably worries that she is lacking some essential womanly, sociable quality, that something is amiss with her. 'There was,' Flora adds. 'She was growing up, and growing up, as she feared, into a world that had no use for her. She carried this burden of care for months, not always conscious of it; sometimes she would forget, and in the reaction become noisy and boisterous; but it was always there, pressing down upon her, until the neighbours noticed her melancholy expression and said: "That child looks regular hag-rid".'

Laura finds some consolation out in the fields, and is briefly lifted by the energy of water and tree-branch on a dull November day. But for Flora, a real solution, a way out of the hamlet's claustrophobia and into a world that did have a use for her, wasn't long in arriving.

3. *The Post-Girl: Flora moves on*

In the summer of 1891 (when Flora was fourteen and a half) she was offered a job as a postal assistant in a large village nearby. The invitation came from 'an old girlhood's friend of her mother' Emma's called Dorcas Lane, who ran the village Post Office, adjacent to a blacksmith's shop that Dorcas had inherited. (Her real name was Kezia Whitton, and again, as with Tom Whiting in 'Candleford', Flora is using a real relative, under a pseudonym, in action which is doubtless a combination of both the real and the imagined.)

In the *Lark Rise* books, the village is called Candleford Green and Flora's account of Laura's time there includes experiences from several Post Offices and towns she got to know. Most probably, she went to work in Fringford, at that time a village in a process of transition. It had a traditional base, with a squire and old houses, but a new housing estate too, for workers who commuted to Buckingham, seven miles away. The expanding, socially mixed population enabled the village to support amenities unknown in the hamlet: a doctor, a fishmonger, a baker's where a plaster-of-paris model of a three-tiered wedding cake stood in the window, and a fashionable dress-shop, run by the Pratt sisters.

The Post Office was the hub of the village, and Dorcas was the village matriarch, or perhaps *patronne*. Flora sketches in Dorcas's character through an extended costume analysis: '. . . not a tall woman and was slightly built, but an erect carriage, a commanding air, and the rustle as she walked of the rich silks she favoured gave her what was then known as a "presence" . . . That afternoon, over a deep prune-coloured gown, she wore a small black satin apron embroidered almost to stiffness with jet beads, and, in accordance with fashion, her still luxurious black hair was plaited into a coronet above a curled fringe.' But a photograph of Dorcas's real-life counterpart, Kezia, standing outside the smithy and taken in about 1890, gives a different impression. It shows a stout and formidable figure (Kezia was reputedly eighteen stone in weight), wearing a voluminous gown and holding the head of a carthorse. Her husband John is standing beside the cart. (He died in 1891, which is probably the reason Flora was invited to come and help at the Post Office.)

Regardless of Kezia/Dorcas's appearance (and much later Flora admitted she had used more than one postmistress as her model), she is a sophisticated woman, then in her mid-fifties. She introduces Laura to refinement and to a lifestyle more luxurious than anything she has experienced in her life so far. Dorcas takes what she calls her evening 'canary dip' in 'a large, shallow, saucer-shaped bath in her bedroom in a few inches of warm rain water well laced with *eau de cologne*'. She allowed Laura *two* eggs for her tea on the day she arrived, an unprecedented treat. Her house is full of an eclectic array of books – Cowper's poems, a complete set of Shakespeare, texts on history and astronomy, and Darwin's *Origin of Species*, which may have become one of Laura's favourites. There is also, more dangerously, a copy of Byron's satirical epic, *Don Juan*. Dorcas makes it clear that this is the one book Laura must not borrow – so of course she does, sneaking it into her room at night and reading it by candlelight. Dorcas also introduces Laura to the library facilities at the Mechanics' Institute at Candleford. Laura takes out a ticket, and 'within a year' she boasts she has worked her way through Dickens, Trollope and Jane Austen.

Laura's duties at the Post Office are limited to start with, though first she has to sign an official declaration of loyalty to Her Majesty's Service before the local squire and magistrate, Sir Timothy, at his hall. She is given responsibility for sorting the mail, and then working behind the counter, selling stamps, distributing forms and receiving parcels. Contrary to Flora's account in *Candleford Green*, there was no telegraph machine at the office when Laura arrived. One was installed a year or so later, and Dorcas covered it at night under a large velvet tea-cosy, as if it were a pet bird.

Laura lived above the shop, and was part of a curious and eclectic household. The two workers at the smithy lodged there, and joined Dorcas and Laura for meals. There were other formidable women: Zillah, the ageing maid who lived in, and the doughty Mrs Macey, who delivered the post, and was regularly around the house. Laura, both in and out of the Post Office, begins to meet a new gaggle of village characters, who are duly logged in her memory banks: army pensioners, evangelical non-conformists, disaffected aristocrats, the aspiring, lower middle-class families who lived in the villas (a new species of person for Laura), and 'Luney Joe', who had a severe learning disability. She makes acquaintances at the village's entertainment evenings: Mr Greenwood, the star performer at the monthly Penny Readings for his histrionic renderings of Dickens; Godfrey Parrish, a visiting journalist (and possible time-traveller from Flora's future short stories) who walks her home one night from a Church social. Laura took fastidious care over her appearance for these events, and topped-off the 'cream nun's veiling frock in which she had been confirmed' with a voguish 'Alexandra' fringe, popularized by the Princess of Wales. This involved cutting the hair above the forehead and tight-curling or frizzing it back towards the crown. In lieu of proper curling-tongs, Laura used a clay pipe she had borrowed from one of the smiths and heated up in a candle flame. In the summer she took to wearing 'softs', the popular name for plimsolls.

Flora sums up Laura's adolescent progress rather curtly: 'A sudden chance glimpse of animal corruption caused her to dwell for weeks on the fate of the human body. She fell into hero-worship of an elderly nobleman and thought it was love. If he noticed her at all, he must have thought her most attentive and obliging over his post-office business. She never saw him outside the office. She learned to ride a bicycle, took an interest in dress, formed her own taste in reading, and wrote a good deal of bad verse which she called "poetry".'

She might well have become stuck in this lowly clerical job, perhaps made it her life. But one day Mrs Macey, the letter-carrier, has a family crisis, and Laura is commandeered to deliver the post. It is a day of deep frozen snow, and Flora has to walk out through it to Sir Timothy's mansion. The sense of privilege of that moment, and the feeling of first-footing in a landscape transformed into two dimensions by the snow and a soft, low 'feather-bed' sky, imprinted itself on her.

Laura delivered the mail regularly after that, and the experience, while it made her work more rewarding, more importantly widened her horizons, and increased her confidence. When, during a brief relationship, a young gamekeeper assumes that Laura is 'his girl', and takes it for granted that she can take a few days off to visit his family, she politely declines and ditches him.

*

Laura begins to grow up in Candleford Green. She learns a trade skill. She has, for a short while, a boyfriend. She reads prodigiously – not just Byron but *Tit-Bits*. She hears almost the entire village singing and whistling Lottie Collins's 'all conquering' hit song, 'Ta-ra-ra-boom-de-ay!' Forty years on, Flora would look back at this moment in her life, and at that new class of people who had left village life for ever – the burgeoning urban and suburban lower middle class – and ponder the future. She did not much like the way they had surrendered to the 'mass standardization of a new civilization', but, equally, did not want rural life to be mired in the past, and hoped they might adapt 'the best of the new to their own needs while still retaining those qualities and customs which have given country life its distinctive character'. 'The choice,' the adult Flora concludes, 'would have to be made.'

But as a young woman she seemed to have already made the choice. Flora lived and worked at Fringford Post Office for six years, and then, 'driven . . . by the restless longing of youth to see and experience the whole of life', she left her home countryside for ever, to spend the rest of her life among the villas of the lower middle class.

*

For twelve months after leaving Fringford, Flora Timms effectively vanished. She had no official status as a clerk, so doesn't figure in the Post Office's employment records, though hints in her books about Laura's progress suggest Flora spent this time doing holiday-relief postal work in various parts of the south-east. But it's clear she had already begun to move decisively away from her Oxfordshire roots, in what has the look of a Victorian gap-year. In the next 'Laura' book (*Heatherley*), she refers briefly to spending time in Essex. She watched her first moving picture in Halstead, near Colchester, in 1898, beginning an enthusiasm for what was 'to become one of the most popular and remunerative arts of the twentieth century', and which was to have a perceptible effect on the dynamics and sense of perspective in her writing.* In the same year she had her first glimpse of the liminal landscapes of the seashore close by: '. . . an Essex saltmarsh bluish mauve with sea lavender, and a tidal river with red fisher sails upon it and gulls wheeling overhead and seaweed clinging to the stones of its quays'.

Along the way, she became familiar with the single-needle telegraph system, which, unlike the machine in Fringford, used Morse code. This qualified her to take charge of a small sub-Post Office, and in the summer of 1898, aged twenty-one, she spotted an advertisement for an assistant's job in the office at Grayshott in Hampshire. This was a long stretch from the Timmses' home country, and it's unlikely that this was a random choice, a pin stuck in the classified columns. The Hampshire weald and Surrey borderlands were charged literary country. William Cobbett was born in Farnham, and toured the area widely in the late eighteenth century. Jane Austen's Chawton was just twenty miles from Grayshott. Selborne – Gilbert White's *Natural History* of the village later enthralled Flora with its idea of the parish as a community of all creatures – was even closer. Grayshott itself was at

---

* The film she saw was entitled *Morning and Night*, the morning scene being of a wedding party emerging from church, and 'Night' featuring a bedroom with 'the bride performing a kind of strip tease act . . . while the bridegroom peered round the edge of a screen, the whole moving in a flickering jig which dazzled the eye of the beholder'.

the hub of a colony of progressive intellectuals nicknamed the Hilltop Writers, which included Bernard Shaw and Arthur Conan Doyle. The aura of this territory must have been seductive to a young person who had grown up with such a passion for literature, offering the chance of touching the hems of the famous, of scenting how it all happened, how books *became*. Whatever Flora's motivation, as a hopeful pilgrim or an adventurous young woman just hoping to spread her wings, she decided to apply. Her six years of Post Office experience and new technical skill must have counted, as she landed the job and took the first step in her crucial move west.

What happened to Flora over the next two years is recalled, and doubtless extensively reworked, in *Heatherley* (Heatherley is her name for Grayshott), the fourth volume in which Laura is reintroduced as the chief subject of the story. But Laura's role in this book is different. She is now in her early twenties, an adult observer, and the distinctions (usually quite clear in the *Lark Rise* trilogy) between Flora's reflective memories and young Laura's vivid child's-eye view, are more obscure. For much of *Heatherley* we seem to be viewing the story through Laura's eyes and feelings. She is both the principal character and Flora's ventriloquial narrator. This makes for a frustrating and detached story at times, as the wide-eyed innocence which adds such a sparkle to the twelve-year-old Laura's view of things becomes rather tiresome when grafted onto a young woman.

But despite (or perhaps because of) its lapses into preciousness, and marginal unreliability as autobiography, *Heatherley* provides a glimpse into Flora's developing imagination and into the first of the two literary landscapes she was to pass through, the watcher with her face pressed against the lighted window.

Laura arrives in Hampshire in the middle of a September heat-wave. She's travelled down by train, pausing for a shopping spree in London to buy clothes, and her new employer, the postmaster George Hertford (in reality a Mr Walter Chapman), was supposed to meet her at Haslemere station, with a pony-drawn 'governess-cart'. But he fails to turn up, and Laura opts to walk the four miles to Heatherley instead. The path takes her through steep and sunken sandstone tracks, and across a scorched heathland of birch and bracken, an unfamiliar land-scape of intense detail and warping perspectives. 'From where she stood she could see, far away on the horizon, a long wavy line of dim blue hills which to her, used as she was to a land of flat fields, appeared to be mountains.'

But there are matters of self-image on Laura's mind, too. This journey is a rite of passage, and she falls back on the reassurance of adaptive camouflage. 'She was dressed in a brown woollen frock with a waist-length cape of the same material and a brown beaver hat decorated with two small ostrich tips, set upright in front, back to back, like a couple of notes of interrogation. This outfit, which would no doubt appear hideous to modern eyes, had given her great moral support on her train journey. The skirt, cut short just to escape contact with the ground, and so needing no holding up except in wet weather, was, her dressmaker had assured her, the latest idea for country wear. The hat she had bought on her way through London that morning. It had cost nine and eleven-pence three farthings of the pound she had saved to meet her expenses until her first month's salary was due in her new post, but she did not regret the extravagance, for it became her brown eyes and hair and would help her, she hoped, to make a good impression at her journey's end. "A good first impression is half the battle", she had been told as a child . . .'

The exactness – and fittingness – of the details in this description are telling: the cape and beaver hat that give the sense of a backwoodswoman; the joshing reference to the ostrich feathers as 'notes of interrogation' to disarm any suspicion of haughtiness or ostentation . . . Fortunately, as she had guessed, her eye-catching fashion-wear also turns out to be sensibly practical, as the long trek to her new home is dusty, hot and physical. The landscape is a revelation. The smell of it, the resins of birch and pine and the warm marzipan of bracken; the sheer fact of *elevation*, the sudden appearance and disappearance of vistas, of dells, dips, thickets, immense spreads of uncultivated common land . . . Compared to the enclosed and niggard fieldscapes she had grown up in, with their 'moist, heavy, pollen-laden air' it seems like a promised land.

And there was the matter of the heather. She knew about the drama of purple-clad moorland from Sir Walter Scott's novels, but had never seen the plant herself, or imagined that it grew in the south country. Now the drifts of purple flowers, 'veined with the gold of late flowering gorse' and alive with bees, gave her a 'buoyant floating-upon-air feeling'. Purple and mauve were to remain emotionally potent colours for her.

After this, Laura's first glimpse of Heatherley is something of an anti-climax, and rather bewildering. It was a type of settlement that she hadn't experienced before. Candleford Green had been bigger, but had a traditional core. Heatherley was almost entirely newly built, a middle-class, suburban village which was fast evolving into a small town. The Post Office she was bound for lay in the centre of the village, and she walked to it through clusters of smart pine-shaded villas and lowly Victorian terraces, a suburban medley of the kind she was to spend many of her future years amidst.

*

In 1876 (the year of Flora's birth) the real village of Grayshott had a population of about a hundred. By the time Laura arrived twenty-two years later, it had grown to seven hundred. Most of the residents were not rural people in the traditional sense, and certainly not land-workers, but first-generation commuters, plus an assortment of writers, artists and fellow travellers escaping from the horrors of an increasingly polluted London. They had at their service not just the telegraph at Grayshott Post Office, but the new railway connection with the capital, which had opened in 1859. The service occupations listed in *Kelly's Directory* for 1899 include many that would have been unknown in Flora's corner of rural Oxfordshire, and catch the character of the new village. There was a fruiterer, a wine merchant, a tobacconist, a confectioner, a bookseller, a purveyor of fishing flies and a cycle agent. In *Heatherley*, Laura (speaking clearly as Flora this time) momentarily forgets she is a new immigrant herself and laments the fact that these traders lacked the pride in their work of 'old-fashioned' shopkeepers, and that Heatherley's new villagers had 'broken with their own personal past and come to a place without traditions, [and] appeared to live chiefly for the passing moment'.

Thomas Wright echoed this in an 1898 guidebook. He was a hack travel writer, and little more than a tourist in the area, but felt qualified to mock the new villagers' poor taste: 'Grayshott looks like a doll's village, not so much because of the size of the houses, but because of their quaintness. The upper storeys are covered with lozenge-shaped bright red tiles, made at Haslemere. It has a temporary look, and there is the feeling that one could upset it like a village built with a pack of cards.'

The Post Office was one of these tiled buildings, and was where Laura would lodge as well as work. She arrives, dust-covered and sweaty and not making the 'good first impression' she had hoped to. But her employer wasn't about, and instead it was an apologetic Mrs Hertford (clearly based on Mrs Chapman, the postmaster's wife) who shows her to her room. This is in a class above Laura's previous digs, indicative of 'people of some refinement'. But she finds it gloomy. There is just one window, reinforced with a screen of painted glass, which casts a dim opalescence into the room. The walls are sage-green. A massive oak cabinet, in faux-Jacobean style, almost fills one wall. The rest of the furniture is also heavily carved, and Laura learns later that it had been made by her employer, a postmaster by title, but a cabinet-maker by trade. In her childhood Laura had shown a penchant for the gothic, where her dreams of hidden retreat met her love for the extravagances of the past. But she affects to find this dark and woody cell, in its 'doll's village', not so much romantic as oppressively sinister. Perhaps this is how Flora remembers feeling, settling into digs a long way from home. But there is a suspicion that she is preparing the stage – lowering the lighting, in effect – for an act of shocking melodrama that was to take place in the house a couple of years later.

When Laura starts work in the Post Office the next day, the omens are hardly more encouraging. She was taking over from a woman in her forties, an ex-employee of the Central Telegraph Office in London, who had been invalided out on a small pension after an attack of nerves. Laura's verdict on her strained face is that she is on the verge of a second breakdown.

One aggravator of her stress is the state of the Hertfords' marriage. She confides in Laura that the couple had furious rows, some of which came close to violence. They had had a serious set-to just before Laura's arrival, which is the reason Mr Hertford failed to meet the train.

Laura, officially, is 'in charge of the office'. She has responsibility for postal and telegraph duties, and for making up the daily accounts. She isn't required to go out on deliveries (no privilege, as far as she was concerned, as it meant she was deprived of the opportunity to go walking in office hours). She has a junior, an eighteen-year-old village girl called Alma, whom she has to initiate into the mysteries of the telegraph machine. (Its incoming Morse code messages needed to be deciphered from the tones emitted by a needle striking two metal sounders, dash on one, dot on the other.) Laura describes Alma as 'pretty, blue-eyed, sweet natured', and found her optimistic and outgoing personality an antidote to her own bouts of moodiness.

Alma has another useful asset. She knows something about poetry, as a consequence of attending a Sunday afternoon class at the house where her father is a gardener. Not, the rather arch Laura makes clear, 'the work of the great poets or that of the more robust type of lesser poet, [but the] smaller, more exquisite things with a touch of magic or faery about them'. Alma introduces Laura to the work of the Pre-Raphaelites Christina Rossetti and Coventry Patmore, the next stage in the long process of literary self-education that Flora had embarked on ten years before.

4. The Hilltop Writers: a spell in rural Bohemia

There was raffish literary company to be had in Grayshott, even for a postal assistant. The Post Office was a point of call for that extraordinary collection of scribes, the so-called Hilltop Writers, who had decamped to the countryside around Hindhead during the 1880s and 90s. In 'Heatherley' they use the Post Office as an informal salon. What Laura had called 'the more robust type of lesser poet' came in to post off their manuscripts. Bernard Shaw held court with his acolytes while leaning on Laura's counter. She had spotted him out walking on her first free Sunday, 'a tall man on a crutch [he had injured himself in a cycling accident] with a forked red beard and quick, searching eyes, surrounded by a group of younger men who appeared to be drinking in every word'.

The sketches of some very well-known writers who did business in the Post Office are amongst the better passages in *Heatherley*. They are never mentioned by name, but are easily recognizable from the descriptions in the book, and from what is known about the literary inhabitants of the region in the 1890s. Laura isn't overawed by her eminent visitors. 'Some of them were brilliant conversationalists and when two or more friends and neighbours met there it amused her to listen to their talk. She would sometimes wish that one of those quick, clever remarks they tossed like coloured glass balls into the air could have come her way, for in her youthful vanity she persuaded herself that she could have caught and returned it more neatly than someone to whom it was addressed.' But in reality Laura is too self-effacing to join in the chit-chat, and believed she was looked on as no more than an extension of the telegraph machine. Her vignettes' occasional darts of reputation-pricking feel as if they are Flora's way of giving her young self a slap on the wrist when she lapses into adulation.

The squire of the Hilltop literary parish was Arthur Conan Doyle. He had, Laura recounts, recently had a big success (with Sherlock Holmes), and had made 'a great impression on the villagers; not so much by his literature as by the big fancy-dress ball he had given at the new hotel on the hill to celebrate it. Scarcely a day passed without his bursting like a breeze into the Post Office, almost filling it with his fine presence and the deep tones of his jovial voice . . . He was probably the most popular man in the neighbourhood.'

Laura is even more breathless about the spectacle of the decadent young poet Richard Le Gallienne, one of Aubrey Beardsley's *fin de siècle* school, as 'he raced about the parish at all hours on his bicycle with his halo of long, fair hair uncovered and his almost feminine slightness and grace set off by a white silk shirt, big artist's bow and velvet knickerbockers.' As for Grant Allen, his 'problem' novel about free-love, *The Woman Who Did* (1895), may have scandalized Victorian society, but not the good people of Heatherley, who showed 'a burning desire to read his book and copies were bought and handed round until practically everyone of mature age in the village had read and passed judgement on it'.

Laura confines herself to remarking on the innocent appearance of the demonized author, a 'quiet-looking little gentleman with the neat grey beard and the field-glasses slung over his shoulder'. She says nothing about the content and themes of his book or those of any of the other local writers, and seems content to bask in their celebrity, clucking at herself from time to time for believing she could ever be part of their world. Perhaps the young Flora felt no interest in them beyond their fame, or that their work was too fast and fashionable to merit the same kind of respect as the classics she doted on. Or perhaps, as a more discriminating adult, looking back, she felt they lacked the authenticity of 'real' country people. Whatever the reason, it is an odd omission. Flora doesn't hold back from making retrospective comments on public affairs later in *Heatherley*, and given that interest in 'a return to the land' continued unabated until she wrote *Lark Rise* forty years later, it's curious that she made no overt connection between the Hilltop Writers' work and her own. Even as a sixty-year-old professional she was dogged by artistic modesty and social awkwardness and a kind of political diffidence. But it would have been remarkable if her developing imagination didn't respond – even if by no more than osmosis – to the social and cultural assumptions that underpinned the Hilltop community.

*

The hills of the Surrey–Hampshire borderlands had begun to attract artists and writers in the 1860s. A group called 'The New Crusade' had set up base in Haslemere and proposed a movement 'back to the land'. They planned to work towards 'the restoration of country life in place of the modern manufacturing town and of country crafts instead of mechanical industries'. The individuals who settled the hills may not have had this degree of philosophical commitment but they were on the same wavelength. One of the first was the watercolourist Myles Birket Foster, whose idyllic portraits of English village life still adorn rustic bric-a-brac. He settled in Witley, near

Godalming, and was soon followed by Helen Allingham, who had made her name illustrating Thomas Hardy's *Far from the Madding Crowd*. In 1866 she exhibited a collection of water-colours of local cottages. The catalogue notes, with regret, that the original buildings were falling into ruin, partly as a result of modern sanitary requirements, but also because their trademark red roof-tiles were themselves migrating, to ornament expanding new settlements like Grayshott.

In 1869 the area's cachet was boosted when Alfred Tennyson and his family moved into a mansion just south of Haslemere. The poet had been complaining about the aggravating sprawl of new buildings around his house on the Isle of Wight, and was directed to the new frontier of the Surrey Hills by the writer and literary fixer Anne Gilchrist, who had just completed her late husband's biography of William Blake and already lived nearby at Shottermill. Two years later, Gilchrist leased her own house to George Eliot (Marian Evans) and her partner George Lewes. This was the kind of social dominoes by which the Hills were colonized, and the eminence of each new arrival confirmed the location's credentials as both a desirable and a practical refuge. Here it was possible to live the rural dream in unimpeachably pure English air, and still be in Bloomsbury in less than two hours.

The man who was to become the theorist of the Hills' virtues, promoting them as a kind of spa for the mind, arrived a few years later. In 1883 John Tyndall set up camp with his wife in a primitive hut they'd built on high ground near Hindhead. Tyndall was an eminent scientist, with a gift for popularizing his discoveries. His most original work was in meteorology. He investigated the absorptive properties of the atmosphere, and how its opacity was changed by heat. He devised a brilliant series of experiments to explain the blueness of the sky, and discovered that organic vapours in the air were precipitated (and therefore dissipated) by bright sunlight. He was the first scientist to describe the now infamous 'greenhouse effect' by which gaseous pollutants (including excess carbon dioxide) warmed up the atmosphere. Persuaded perhaps by his discoveries of the refining nature of mountain air, he kept a house in the Swiss Alps, and achieved a second cloak of renown as a climber. A portrait photograph from 1888 (by Herbert Barraud) suggests a visionary ascetic, with a full, white fringe-beard, like an Amish elder. The would-be Parnassians of Surrey may not have appreciated the fine details of Tyndall's work, but they knew his thesis about the purity of high air, and that he'd dubbed the ridge of sandstone slopes between Hindhead and Haslemere (which reach the dizzying height of 400 metres) 'the English Switzerland'.

From about 1890 the trickle of incomers became an avalanche. Grant Allen built a house close to the Devil's Punch Bowl in 1893, and in prose as evangelical as his radical fiction, explained the deep attractions of the hill country. It was a perfect and prescient summary of rural longing, and of the myth of the good life. 'I am writing in my study on a heather-clad hilltop. When I raise my eye from my sheet of foolscap, it falls upon miles and miles of broad open moorland. My window looks out upon unsullied nature. Everything around is fresh and clean and wholesome. Through the open casement, the scent of pines blows in with the breeze from the neighbouring firwood. Keen airs sough through the pine-needles. Grasshoppers chirp from deep tangles of bracken. The song of the skylark drops from the sky like soft rain in summer ... But away below in the valley, as night draws on, a lurid glare reddens the north-eastern horizon. It marks the spot where the great wen of London heaves and festers. Up here on the free hills, the sharp air blows in upon us, limpid and clear from a thousand leagues of open ocean; down there in the crowded town, it stagnates and ferments, polluted with the diseases and vices of centuries.'

A throng of writers (perhaps the collective term for starlings – a 'murmuration' – might be usefully borrowed here) were living in the hills by the end of the nineteenth century. The classicist George Gilbert Murray had settled at Barford, and become the model for Shaw's character Adolphus Cusins in *Major Barbara*. Sir Francis Galton, polymathic scientist and explorer, moved house as regularly as a modern celebrity, and spoke of 'that wonderful air-cure Hindhead' – though his advocacy of human eugenics was anathema to the social reformers Sidney and Beatrice Webb, ensconced nearby at Bramshott. The philosopher Bertrand Russell, the most celebrated atheist of his time, lived a short bike ride from the theological writer Hannah Pearsall Smith,* who was as devout in her religion as her feminism.

Women's rights were the most hotly contested issue among the Hilltoppers and one of the few subjects they openly debated among themselves. George Eliot, H. G. Wells and (ambivalently) Grant Allen lined up as feminist fellow-travellers, while Christina Rossetti and the novelists Mary Humphry Ward and Margaret Oliphant (author of *Miss Marjoribanks*) came out vehemently against women's suffrage. It cannot have made for a very neighbourly atmosphere amongst the curative breezes.

---

* Russell eventually married Hannah's younger daughter Alys, much to Hannah's disgust. At the Annual Council of the British Women's Temperance Association she proposed the motion: 'Resolved that it is the sense of this Council that all men should be castrated'.

Indeed, the collective noun 'colony' for this motley collection of free-thinkers and dogmatists, faddists and sybarites, crafts-men, nouveau-riche industrialists, visionary scientists and bewhiskered antiquarians, is almost as wishful as the epithet 'school' would have been. Beyond the bewildering variety of earnest 'isms' they individually supported, the Hilltoppers shared only two things in common: a belief that living in the country was practically and spiritually beneficial; and a belief that frequent departures from it to the stimulations of the town were an essential complement – or at least a way of translating the rural experience into career opportunities. This was pretty much the delicate balancing act that Flora was working out in her own life, however unconsciously.

The Hilltop Writers did manage to collaborate on two typi-cal Victorian projects. The first was the creation of the Haslemere Microscope and Natural History Society (on whose membership lists Flora herself appears during a later sojourn in the area). The development of comparatively cheap micro-scopes in the middle of the nineteenth century added a new dimension to Victorian natural history. They made it possible for even the humblest creatures and plants to join the cornu-copia of organisms which demonstrated the wisdom and inventiveness of the creator. Diminutive size, apparent insig-nificance, even outright drabness were all revealed through the lens to shroud a whole world of delicacy and intricate design.

The bestselling gardening writer James Shirley Hibberd saw the magnified frondery of ferns as 'vegetable jewellery . . . plumy emerald green pets glistening with health and beadings of warm dew'. Nature's silent majority were emerging into daylight. The Victorians rarely missed an opportunity to see moral parables in nature, and naturalists such as the banker J. E. Bowman would have been well aware of the metaphorical significance of what – trembling 'in an ecstasy of delight' – he witnessed through his lenses: 'How many beautiful and interesting productions', he wrote, 'we tread daily underfoot and pass by unnoticed.' Flora was later to make metaphorical use in *Heatherley* of small natural history cameos (for example of ecological food-chains and the importance of the small, hard-working organisms at the bottom) which she rather unconvincingly attributes to Laura.

The Haslemere MNHS had its origins in an evening class started by Colonel William Mason in 1888, to help working men study nature with the help of a microscope. Such 'Mechanics Institutes' flourished at the end of the nineteenth century, especially in the big cities. Out in the rural provinces they soon evolved into clubs for middle-class professionals, and in the elevated atmosphere of the Surrey Hills into a highbrow forum for the local intellectuals. Shaw, Tyndall, Grant Allen, Conan Doyle and Gilbert Murray were all enthusiastic members of the Society and took part in its debates.

The natural retreat for refreshment after a vigorous discussion of the oddity of mosses or '120 Years of Non-conformity in Haslemere' was the Fox and Pelican, a bespoke public house the Colony had built in its own earnest image. In 1898, a local brewer threatened to set up a conventional pub in the centre of Grayshott. At the time there was a moral panic about the dangers of drunkenness among the working classes, and societies were springing up devoted to establishing Temperance Houses. Bernard Shaw was vegetarian and teetotal himself, but didn't agree with the uncompromising aims of the temperance movement. In collaboration with the Church Commissioners and local supporters, he helped set up the Grayshott and District Refreshment House Association, to provide an alternative refuge where workers could take a well-earned drink at the end of the day in respectable and tempering (if not quite temperate) surroundings. They succeeded in finishing the build of the Fox and Pelican that year, intending to run it on what was known as the 'Gothenburg system', i.e. as a non-profit-making place of refreshment and entertainment for families, in which the consumption of alcoholic drinks was permitted, but not encouraged. There would be a limited number of light beers available, and coffee and food too.

The name was chosen by Sir Frederick Pollock, legal scholar, literary mountaineer (another of a significant chapter of climbers base-camped in the Surrey Hills), and one of the first settlers in Hindhead. He had been to Corpus Christi College in Oxford, whose heraldic device is a pelican and whose founder was Bishop Fox. (Doubtless the improving parable of 'the pelican in its piety' – the devoted family bird pecking its own breast to give reviving but non-inebriating blood to its young – was also at the back of his mind.) Shaw donated a large collection of books to establish a bar-room library. The Arts and Crafts designer Walter Crane, a friend of Shaw's, painted the sign. The whole enterprise was a symbol of the Colony's high-mindedness – except that, by all accounts, moderation at the bar fell quickly by the wayside.*

Laura visits the Fox and Pelican occasionally, but until Alma had learned to use the telegraph machine, she couldn't leave the office at lunchtime. So she enrolled the telegraph

---

* The Fox and Pelican continues to trade, though now as a conventional pub. Inside there is a noticeboard with a brief history of the inn's exotic origins, and a longer account of its sporting prowess. The pub was the base of the Grayshott Cricket Club, and Conan Doyle was one of their star batsmen. He scored 37 in a key match against Linchmere in July 1903, and Grayshott went on to win. The building which housed the Post Office still survives too, amid a plethora of oriental take-aways. Flora would be gratified to see that it now houses a shop devoted to stylish women's clothes.

messenger boy to fetch her the cheap dinners that were a feature of the new model inn. ('It was an immense nine-pennyworth and included a thick cut off the joint, two or more vegetables, and a wedge of fruit tart or a round of roly-poly, sufficient for three dinners for one with her appetite'). She also goes to hear the local writers read from their books, and deliver their pronouncements on spiritualism, the Boer War, the Balkan Problem and the even more vexing Women Problem. Most often she went to hear the red-bearded Shaw's charismatic lectures on socialism (though she doesn't mention the occasion Shaw and Richard Le Gallienne spoke at the local school, and caused consternation among the staff by instructing the pupils that 'The first duty of a child is to disobey its parents, and grown-ups generally').

Laura makes no more reference to the effects on her of such a maelstrom of radical and eccentric ideas than she does to the contents of the Hilltop Writers' books. All that seeps through in *Heatherley* is the heavily underlined contrasting of their high intellects with her literary inadequacy and humble ambition, plus the faintest zest of sour grapes. She admits that encountering these living authors made her as star-struck as 'a good view of a living film star would . . . to many girls of today'.

Much later in her life Flora was to reflect more cynically on this literary hero-worship. 'I used to listen to [their] conversation . . . meeting and greeting each other at my counter, myself as unregarded as a piece of furniture, but noting all. Perhaps these "great examples" encouraged my desire to express myself in writing, but I cannot remember the time when I did not wish and mean to write. My brother and I used to make up verses and write stories and diaries from our earliest years, and I had never left off writing essays for the pleasure of writing. No one saw them; there was no one likely to be interested.'

But in *Heatherley*, Laura confesses that the heady literary air humbles her into abandoning the journal 'begun on the day she first left home . . . She had destroyed that with her other scraps of writing, saying to herself as they smouldered to tinder that that was the end of a foolish idea.' But this theatrical gesture was no more than a fit of the sulks, and Laura's childhood ambition (and 'pleasure') soon reasserts itself. '[A]fter the folly had been renounced, there remained with her a sense of some duty neglected which almost amounted to a feeling of guilt, a feeling which persisted throughout her life whenever her pen was idle.' And it impels her to take another fan's outing (to burn incense at the shrine, as she put it) to George Meredith's house in Box Hill (some twenty miles from Grayshott), a writer whose flamboyantly romantic prose and perceptiveness about women were very much to her taste.

The only surviving photograph of the young Flora dates from this time. It's a professional portrait, taken against a soft background, and with a little darkroom enhancement of the swan-like elegance of the subject's neck and the petiteness of her features. It's also in profile, so the rather disproportionately large lips that figure in later snapshots look thin and intelligently determined. The photographer's instinct – or Flora's natural diffidence – has her posed with face tilted slightly downwards and eyes hooded, as if she were in wistful contemplation. Together, photographer and model have conjured up an archetypal portrait of a sensitive, probably artistic woman, who might almost pass for a Romantic beauty if it were not for the fact that her hair is done up in a bun. The effect of the tightly wound top-knot is to balance the slight neediness in the face with blue-stocking seriousness – a contrariness which Flora recognized in herself, for all her demurrals.*

Even if she believed she was regarded as a 'piece of furniture', outside and ignored by the literary clique, she and her friends could at least play at being Bohemians. The young girls of that time (they had what today would be called a 'lifestyle' magazine called *The Girl of Today*) saw themselves as creatures of the *fin de siècle* – unconventional, emancipated, and with a freedom to speak and think for themselves inconceivable to their mothers. But in the countryside such ideas had filtered through in a diluted or symbolic way. Laura's set were 'the daughters of shopkeepers, shop assistants and other business girls, whose parents kept apartment houses or farmed in a small way', and Laura insists they 'were *fin de siècle* only in the sense of having been born towards the end of the century'. They were well aware of the ridicule heaped on the New Women in the press, the sneers at their androgynous ugliness and demand for ancient male privileges. 'With such a warning before her as the current travesty of the "new woman" the average country girl determined to abstain altogether from ideas and concentrate upon being feminine.'

Laura was, as so often, being disingenuous, and her long descriptions of her own excursions into femininity show how she was always able to express 'ideas' as fashion. She read and interpreted the meaning of current fashions with an acute eye, and if her descriptions of her own clothing are similarly scrutinized, they suggest a cluster of 'ideas' consistent with her

---

* A bronze bust of Flora Thompson, created on the centenary of her birth in 1976, now resides in Liphook Public Library. It was modelled from this single photograph, and transfers into three dimensions the elegant narrowness of face shown in the profile photograph. This sculptural Flora now resembles a classical Muse, and holds a quill pen in her hand.

emerging social philosophy: robust femininity, support for modernism, but a parallel respect for trusted tradition.

She would have been aware of, though made no obvious concessions to, one alternative to the 'New Woman' styles. The last decades of the nineteenth century saw the back-to-the-land (or back-to-simplicities) movement move into the arena of clothing, with an agenda for so-called 'rational dress'. The principles advocated by Rational Dressers (and they had a society, the RDS) were sensible enough, and a reaction against the formality and (sometimes literally) suffocating rigidity of Victorian clothing. They campaigned against hourglass waists and tight-laced corsets, against woollen combinations and heavy drape skirts, and the obligatoriness – even in the garden – of ponderous gloves and hats. Instead they proposed – in the interests of health as well as comfort – lighter, more informal clothes, in which the wearer had freedom to move and breathe. Unfortunately the garments that got their approval were usually brown, shapeless and far from fashionable.

Flora almost certainly saw Rational clothing on some of the Hilltop clan, especially on the angular frame of George Bernard Shaw. He was an enthusiast for wool, and when he was young and impecunious in London, had saved up ten pounds to buy a Jaeger woollen suit in the firm belief that it would keep him healthy for the rest of his life. Dr Gustav Jaeger (who went on to found the clothing chain) was a German physiologist who argued that animal bodies were meant to be kept warm by animal wool, and that the wearing of vegetable fibres like linen and cotton was an unhealthy and unnatural perversity. Jaeger's prescriptions for menswear read like the inventory for a Victorian sanatorium or home for the permanently infantilized, and were a long way from being an improvement on the stiff-collar. The signature garment was the 'sanitary wool shirt', made of stockinette and fastened on the shoulder with a double layer across the chest. Normal trousers were an 'unaesthetic monstrosity' and were replaced by close-fitting knitted leggings held up by sanitary woollen braces.

Laura abhorred anything potentially ugly and unexpressive. During the two years she spent in Heatherley, she put together outfits that were a kind of Victorian precursor of Laura Ashley, by combining the more acceptable bits of informal Rational Dress and New Woman modes. Out walking, she donned flower-wreathed hats, floating scarves and frilly muslin frocks. They were long enough to 'sweep up the dust' and (was this her closet intention, to entangle her town and country selves?) 'catch and tear on the bushes'. For work, she dressed smartly. She slept in curlers with her face plastered with cold cream, and put on regulation serge skirts and cotton tops: 'the blouses made with stiff, stand-up collars and worn with a tie. In this attire she flattered herself that she looked very neat and businesslike, but she often longed for something softer to the touch and more becoming'.

To achieve this latter look she went to the expense of getting frocks made by a professional dressmaker, which meant she could afford just one new dress a year. Except that, in that 'reckless hour' she had gone shopping in London on her move down to Heatherley, she had spent two guineas on a tailor-made grey coat and skirt, which she set off with a birthday present from an aunt of 'a perfectly toning muff and fur necklet of the then fashionable grey, silky, thickly-curling fur called Thibet'. So the village girl challenged the restraints of her origins with *haute couture*. But Laura hadn't yet got the self-confidence to ape the women cyclists who poured through the local countryside at the weekends. They wore a piece of kit which had evolved from a marriage between Rational Dress and chic fashion. Viscountess Harberton, a leading light in the RDS, had designed an early *culotte*, a divided skirt which was only half a yard around at the ankles. The women cyclists developed this into a garment which, Laura accurately but somewhat sniffily relates, had 'some kind of cleavage for riding, but fell to the feet in folds when the rider dismounted'.

*

Whether Flora felt the kind of slight alienation from her *fin-de-siècle* companions that Laura's dispassionate account suggests – the sense that she is acting in a play without any real conviction that she has been cast in the right role – is hard to say. The urge to write is still smouldering somewhere inside her, though without any tangible outcomes. So is the urge to be fashionable, as if this might provide another way of expressing herself, as well as a more obvious key to social acceptability for someone who still remembered her childhood awkwardness. The two compulsions don't sit easily together. They represent a duality that runs through Flora's life, one half of her mind fixed dreamily on the future, the other trying to make the best of where she is, and the baggage of her origins; trying to relate to friends when intimacy was always a difficult thing for her.

At any rate Laura was soon drifting away from the *fin-de-siècle* girls and making some unlikely new acquaintances. One was the character she names as 'Mr Foreshaw' (his name perhaps an obscure pun), a 'distinguished-looking old gentleman with snow-white hair and a small, neatly-trimmed white beard' who regularly appeared at her Post Office counter. Flora catches his persona in a quick sketch of his clothes: 'In winter he wore a long, thick black overcoat and a sealskin cap with ear-pieces tied down under his chin. In hot summer weather he would sometimes appear in a white drill suit of tropical cut.'

Laura ('loving a mystery, and being exceptionally fond of aged people') becomes intrigued by this veteran of the Empire, despite local gossip that he was a misogynist and employed an elderly ex-serviceman in lieu of a housemaid, and begins to ingratiate herself with him. Disregarding Post Office regulations, she would extract the letters from his arthritic hands and stick the stamps on for him. One August evening, after the office had been shut, she breaks even more rules by personally delivering a telegram to his bungalow just off Heatherley's main street.

She spies Foreshaw (sea-grey dressing gown; black smoking-cap) sitting at a map-draped table, is invited in and offered a drink. When Laura rather timidly says she would like a little water or milk, he replies that 'he had not suspected her of being a milk and watery miss, and milk he had not, never touched the stuff, and as to giving her water, he'd leave that sort of hospitality to good Christian people. He's an old pagan, thought Laura, a regular old pagan, and repeated the word mentally with some pride, for she had but recently discovered its modern usage.'

As their friendship develops over the weeks, the maps, and the red ink-marks scrawled over them, are explained. The old pagan had been a professional big-game hunter for thirty years from the 1860s in British and Portuguese East Africa. The bungalow is stuffed with trophies and exotic bric-a-brac – spears, blowpipes, crocodile skins, a huge elephant tusk from a fatally wounded animal that had almost collapsed on him in its death throes. Laura's usual tenderness for abused wild creatures (and Flora's: she became a vitriolic opponent of hunting in her 1920s journalism) seems absent or suppressed here, except when she is shown a case of tropical butterflies 'with wings of the most glorious colours, as bright and fresh as if newly painted, but with wings and bodies so stiff and motionless and so imprisoned under the glass that the sight made her feel sad. "Pretty things," he said, "you like them, eh?" [Laura] could think of no better answer than, "I should like to see them alive."'

In fact Laura was enchanted by Mr Foreshaw and his stories, which Flora, with her exact memory and decades of familiarity with popular literature, recreates forty-five years later in a convincing imitation (or parody) of a *Boy's Own* adventure tale. 'That was the time I saw with my own eyes the Hindoo kill, pluck and roast a chicken and burn the feathers, then bring it back to life again. Heard the thing's death squawk, saw its blood run when he cut its throat, smelt the roasting flesh and the feathers burning, take my oath I did! Then saw the live fowl running and cackling afterwards. No conjuring about it. Ground as bare as the palm of my hand for yards around and the fellow practically naked. Just him and the bird and a little stick fire. How do I think it was done? Now you're asking something. Some say it's mesmerism. Fowl never killed, and of course never roasted; just a few feathers burnt, and the rest takes place in the imagination of the spectators, suggested by the performer of course.'

Laura was not immune to mesmerism herself. She becomes fond of Mr Foreshaw, and for the best part of a year visits him at least once a week. Over tea, she listens enraptured to his stories of derring-do, and in return he throws off his reputation as a woman-hater by behaving like a favourite uncle, providing her with a private parlour ('a little bower for you if you want to curl your hair or anything') complete with looking-glass and a bottle of eau de cologne. They made an odd pair, the gruff, cosmopolitan ex-colonial, and the self-deprecating, fanciful twenty-two-year-old from rural Oxfordshire, and Alma may not have been the only one in Heatherley to have raised an eyebrow at their relationship. Laura herself believed that no one but Alma knew of her visits, and if they did, 'Mr Foreshaw's great age exempted her from the rule of the day that no really nice girl should ever go alone to the house of a man.'

Flora's explanation for Laura's attachment was that she liked 'his originality, his raciness, his immense store of experience and his biting wit'. But she also clearly enjoyed the presence of a father-figure, and the flattery of a little male attention, of which she seemed to have perilously little, either from local young men or the Parnassians who wafted past her counter. And Mr Foreshaw fitted into the cast of eccentrics – gipsies, bee-women, passing strangers – who had captivated Laura since she was a small girl. He was being filed for future reference.

Laura's reaction when he died in his sleep a year later is a mixture of wry reportage and veiled melancholy. Only his doctor and lawyer attended the funeral, and their 'wired, waxen florist's' wreaths were the only flowers laid on the coffin – except for a bunch of red roses, a tribute from 'another friend' (Flora giving strained anonymity to the obvious donor). There is some black comedy in the description that follows of the auctioning of Foreshaw's belongings. Laura watches through the Post Office window as men trundle the heavy Empire-style furniture home in wheelbarrows and a boy trots past with a pair of African antlers held to his forehead. But she was genuinely saddened by his loss. Despite the deaths of four of her siblings and several village elders back in Lark Rise, she confesses that: 'People she had known had died and she had felt sorry, but none of them had been near to her; she had never before faced the great dark, silent abyss which lies between the dead and the living.'

Flora had opted, from choice and the dictates of her personality, for a largely solitary life, to be an outside observer of others' affairs. Much of Laura's spare time in Heatherley was spent walking the local heathlands, especially the open wastes of Ludshott and Bramshott Commons, which began just a mile to the west of Heatherley/Grayshott. '[I]t took her but a few minutes to reach open country. Looking neither to right nor left lest she should see some acquaintance who would volunteer to come with her, she would rush like a bandersnatch, as someone once said who had seen her from a distance, and take the first turning out of the village which led to the heath.' (On another occasion she was followed by a nosy neighbour, 'just to see who she had met'.) Sometimes she found and watched gipsies, the aboriginals revered by almost all nineteenth-century rural writers, and on other occasions talked to smallholders and a local 'broom-squire', who followed the traditional local craft of making brooms from switches of birch twigs.

Laura was especially fond of Waggoners Wells, a group of man-made lakes on the common which were entirely shrouded by trees, and where, in spring, primroses and wood anemones were reflected in the pale green water.* This was the kind of sequestered bower that had bewitched her as child, and continued to do so as she grew up. On Ludshott Common the alternation of heights and hidden dells affects her with the same

*Waggoners Wells, originally called Wakeners Wells, were once believed to have been hammer-ponds created in connection with a local, wood-fuelled iron-smelting business, but they were never used as such. They're now owned by the National Trust, as is much of the surrounding heath and woodland.

power as her first glimpse of the Surrey landscape a year before, as she'd walked up from Haslemere station. Flora gives Laura the benefit of her long reflection on how landscape shapes the spirit and the writer's eye. 'Her love of her own county was that of a child for its parent, a love which takes all for granted, instinctive rather than inspiring, but lifelong. Her love of the Heatherley countryside was of a different nature. It had come to her suddenly in that moment of revelation when, on the day of her arrival, she had unexpectedly come out on the heath and seen the heather in bloom. She had felt then a quick, conscious sense of being one with her surroundings.' The sense of the homeland as emotional root was being subtly replaced by the idea of landscape as a lexicon of feeling. It is always hard to tell when Flora is putting her adult reflections into Laura's head, but in one *Heatherley* passage the memory is so sensually sharp and metaphorically powerful that I think it truthfully represents what the young Flora Timms felt, and that she was already seeing things through a writer's imagination.

Laura is out for an evening saunter in May, hoping to hear the Ludshott nightingales. She finds a likely site, a dense semi-circle of hawthorns in full blossom, a natural amphitheatre. She waits until twilight, and the May petals drift down onto her face, like unseasonal snowflakes. No nightingales sing, but imperceptibly, as she sits in the shadow of the trees, there comes, first, the heavy, disorientating sound of a bicycle with flat tyres, and then the figure of the rider, a sailor in 'an ordinary bell-bottomed bluejacket'. He is sobbing uncontrollably, and passes her by, as oblivious of her presence as she is of the source of his grief. 'She had gone out to hear nightingales and heard instead the desolate sound of human suffering, and that against a background of pure loveliness.'

*

Just a few months previously, and only six miles to the north, another rural-writer-to-be had also been crouched under a hedge at night, covertly listening in to a conversation between two sweethearts. Like Laura, George Sturt was confused as to what was going on in front of him; unlike her, he was self-consciously agonizing over how to render his experiences in words, and the deeper philosophical problem as to whether such eavesdropping on others' lives was justified. This was how he noted down the experience in his journal:

. . . the talk obscurely drifted (I missed the links) into the girl's narration of her dreaming last night.

'I dreamt you was in there long wi' me, and you was bad. I kep' on astin' ye what I could do, and you wouldn't say. I says, "Shall I git up an boil the kittle," and all you'd say was, "Oh, don't trouble." And so on. You was bad. An' then when I woke up, you wa'n't there.'

The man mumbled, inaudibly to me.

The girl: 'I reckon you was there, somewhere.'

The man: 'Cou'n't ha' bin. I was up 'ere in the mornin', and I never noticed comin'. I must ha' bin purty quick to do that.'

(Did the girl say then, or have I imagined 'If not last night, you must ha' bin there some night. I kep' on dreamin' you was there though?')

The man: 'P'raps it'll be better tonight?'

Sturt owned a wheelwright's business in Farnham, just north of Grayshott, but as far as is known Flora never met him. Nor was he ever part of the Surrey Hills set, despite being a writer and thinker on a par with the best of them. But he is worth a moment's digression because he represents the kind of rural

writer Flora Timms did *not* become. He was born thirteen
years before Flora, and took over the family business in 1890,
aged twenty-seven, after six years teaching at Farnham Gram-
mar School. He began a remarkable journal that year (the
above is an entry for 25 June 1898), which was partly an astrin-
gently striking notebook of weather and nature, partly a series
of sketches of the behaviour of his workers, and partly a deeply
analytical and self-critical account of creativity and what, philo-
sophically, constituted the 'good life'.

He was no better read than Flora, but had read different
things: the American Transcendentalists – Thoreau, Emerson
and Whitman; socialist thinkers such as Henry Salt and William Morris, the aesthete Walter Pater – and his writing
reflected their philosophical approach. He went on to produce
several classic books on south country life at the end of the
nineteenth century, including *The Bettesworth Book* (1901), *Memoirs of a Surrey Labourer* (1907) and *Change in the Village* (1912).
This last book is, in a way, the political sub-text of *Lark Rise to
Candleford* made explicit, and covers similar documentary territory to Flora's books. But the two authors approached their
material in sharply contrasting ways.

Sturt was detached, theoretical, in a state of constant moral
quandary. Like Flora, he used a disguise, the pen-name 'George
Bourne' (after the hamlet just outside Farnham where he grew
up), but this was not so much to hide himself as to protect the
family business, in case his customers might doubt his credibil-
ity as a wheelwright's shop manager if they discovered he was
also a secret scribbler. Unlike Flora he did not begin life as one
of the people he wanted to describe, and his accounts of rural
workers always have the diligent, cold objectivity of the visiting sociologist. Perhaps that is a good thing; Sturt would never
have dreamed of fictionalizing, or even dressing up, his charac-

ters in the way Flora did. But without imaginative empathy, his laborious attempts at, for instance, rendering rural dialects literally (as above), ended, as often than not, in patronizing Mummerset. His books were also open political arguments about the virtues, drawbacks and fate of the old organic community. Flora's writing explores the same things, yet there are few explicit arguments, just a seepage of feeling from the intense human detail. But Sturt's classic *Change in the Village* appeared twenty-five years before *Lark Rise*, and it helped shape the conversation about rural life that was buzzing in the background all the time Flora was learning her trade as a writer.

5. *The* Fin-de-Siècle *girl*

For Flora in the late 1890s the constraints on her life were practical, not philosophical. In March 1899, a little more than six months after she had arrived in Grayshott, she began to find the turbulent atmosphere in Walter Chapman's house where she was staying intolerable. As she makes Laura discover, the relationship between 'George Hertford' and his wife is plainly in crisis. George flies into increasingly aggressive rages, and Mrs Hertford, like many abused wives, into periods of self-delusion and submissiveness.

Laura sometimes hears him padding softly about the house at night, and once or twice wakes up suddenly with the sense of someone in her room. Things come to a head one night when Laura hears what sounds like an explosion in the house. Out on the landing she finds Mrs Hertford in her nightdress, coaxing her husband back to bed. He has a revolver in his hand. Later Mrs Hertford gives Laura his (or her) rationalization of what had happened. Mr Hertford believed he had heard whispering beneath the landing window, and thinking it might be burglars, had fired a shot to scare them away. Laura confesses that she was scared even if the imagined burglars weren't, and within a week she has packed her bags and moved out.

It was a fortunate exit. Two years later, a few months after she had left Heatherley, Laura learns that Hertford had murdered his wife in sensational circumstances. In July 1901, Walter Chapman, the real-world model for Mr Hertford, had stabbed Mrs Chapman to death while she was bathing their new-born child. At the inquest the local doctor testified to finding twenty-one puncture wounds in the body, and the four-inch-long shank of a carpenter's carving tool so firmly embedded in her back that he had to use pincers to remove it. He also testified that he had been worried about Chapman's mental health since November 1898, when he had begun making accusations about his wife's immorality and assertions that he was being followed. (This, perhaps coincidentally, was just a few weeks after Flora's arrival in the household.) His subsequent trial at Winchester Assizes lasted less than two hours. 'Murder, committed under an uncontrollable impulse' was the jury's verdict. Chapman was declared guilty but insane, and sentenced to indefinite detention in Broadmoor.

The reaction that Flora attributes to Laura when she hears this news is revealing, awarding the melodramatic storyteller precedence over the frightened single woman. Laura envisages the drama of Hertford's arrest as a grand Victorian narrative painting, full of parable and dramatic irony: 'The screaming and rushing to and fro; the village constable suddenly called upon to face what was almost certainly, to him, an unprecedented situation; women running into their houses and locking their doors when they heard a madman was at large . . . then the arrival of the closed carriage which was in use there, to take brides to their weddings and mourners to funerals, and the dazed culprit ushered into it, arm in arm with doctor and policeman, while all the time, but a few yards away, the sun shone on the heather, pine-tops swayed in the breeze, birds sang and bees gathered honey, as on any ordinary summer morning.'

Laura takes time to settle after leaving the Hertfords. She spends a few weeks as a boarder with a retired business couple and their grown-up daughter in a villa just beyond the main street, but doesn't have the privacy she wanted. Then she finds a place wholly to her liking. It is, on the surface, an unpromising and meagre retreat, one room in one half of a small Victorian house. It had been put up for sale by a speculative builder in the hope of attracting 'a superior type of purchaser', but was so poky he was only able to rent it out to a working-class family. 'The Ferns', in a back-street just up the hill from the old Post Office, is a dark, bay-windowed villa that looks as if it has been transplanted from the suburbs of west London, or an H. G. Wells novel. But Laura's upstairs room has two fair-sized windows and a view over the heath, with the line of blue hills she had seen on first arriving in Heatherley just visible in the distance.

What Laura likes about this space of her own says something about the kind of person Flora was becoming: 'The bare room did not strike her as particularly bare: it had a clean bed, a table, primarily for meals, at which she could write, shelves in a recess by the fireplace for her books, a shabby but comfortable old easy-chair, patched on both elbows, and a paraffin lamp which her landlady had bought at an auction sale. Laura thought the lamp, when lighted, gave quite an air to the room with its red, crinkled silk shade and embossed figures on its silver-coloured base. It certainly smelt a little, but when she remarked upon this her landlady told her that she used for it only the best tea-rose lamp-oil and, after that, the name of the brand of oil seemed to sweeten the scent.' *La vie bohème* could be glimpsed even in the scented shadows cast by a cheap oil-lamp.

Laura is so reticent that it is hard to know how she really feels about living alone on a salary of a pound a week. Her friend Kitty remarks that she would 'go "balmy on the crumpet"'*

* An obsolete Victorian and Edwardian slang phrase meaning slightly dotty – used incidentally in print by H. G. Wells, who was a frequent visitor to the Surrey Hills community.

sitting up there with nobody to talk to'. But Laura insists that quiet and solitude are her 'spiritual meat and drink', and if they added to her visible mysteriousness, then that was no bad thing in the mood of the times. She certainly seems to have made few close relationships in Heatherley.

Flora's accounts of some friendships that petered out are among the chapters she chose to omit from her final version of *Heatherley*, though they survive in her papers.* One in particular, entitled 'The Jeromes', was too disparaging of a possibly still-living writer to risk publishing. Flora may also have felt, on reflection, that it gave too ambiguous an impression of her feelings about the craze for all things Bohemian. 'Bohemianism' at the turn of the century was as much a tag for trivial lifestyle choices as a considered alternative philosophy. 'An impromptu picnic, informal manners, an easy, careless style of dress, especially if it included big, loose bows, or bright colours, a friendship between two of opposite sexes, all passed as Bohemian,' Laura explains. '[The term] could be applied to a girl who had appeared in public with a little powder on her nose, to a woman who, having a maid, opened the front door herself to visitors, or to a couple who were living together without marriage, or who starved their servants and beat their children. Any departure from convention, short of punishable crime was Bohemian.'

Laura's first intimate close encounter with Bohemia, beyond the casual, over-the-counter dealings she had with the Hilltop gang, is with a couple who also use her post room. Mr Jerome is a tall man in late middle age with a theatrical accent (in summer he wears a black alpaca jacket and a limp white Panama,

* And are included in the 1998 edition, published by John Owen Smith (see Sources).

and carries a 'large flag basket, such as workmen used at that time'), who works as a small-time writer of short stories. Mrs Jerome is a schoolteacher some twenty years younger than her husband. She was of French birth, 'dressy', blessed with a fading beauty and what Laura describes as '*chic*'. It was a loose quill in one of Mrs Jerome's chic French hats that brought the three of them together, while Mr Jerome was posting off one of his stories. Laura offers her a needle and cotton to repair it and they fall into conversation. Once the ice has been broken they become friendlier with each visit to the Post Office. Soon they are inviting Laura home for tea on Sundays, and introducing her to a style of living beyond her previous experience.

Laura is intrigued by their habits and finds it exciting to sit at a tea-table where the master of the house drinks unsweetened tea from a glass, and the lady smokes. Even more Bohemian, in dress-sensitive Laura's eyes, was the fact that Mrs Jerome – now referred to as Alicia – did sewing on a Sunday. 'When ruching had gone out and tucks were in fashion she would spend a whole Sunday unpicking and pressing and stitching the front of one of her blouses. Then she had her almost weekly millinery bout. Her talent in this line almost amounted to magic. She would take a few square inches of velvet, ruffle, stitch, pat and pull it, stick a quill at one side, or drape it with a veil, then, holding it at arm's length, say "How do you like my new toque?" "Three guineas at Heath's," her husband would say promptly.'

Mr Jerome – his forename was Wilmot – seemed to approach writing in a similarly technical way. Plots were crucial, he insisted, and must be worked out architecturally. He had devised a system of graphs to assist him in this task, and his off-the-peg characters and touches of 'local colour' were slotted into the framework like 'flesh upon what he called the skeleton'. Laura, agog for any insights into the mysterious processes of real writing, found this system impressive, until she read and heard the results. Wilmot was fond of reading aloud at their Sunday afternoon teas, and after his elegant thespian tones had rendered extracts from Dickens, Thackeray and Hardy (with some added 'Victorian mannerisms'), he goes on to read whatever he had written since Laura's last visit. This puts Laura 'in a delicate position'. Although she is flattered to be treated to these first performances, and enjoys seeing Wilmot in a buoyant mood about his creations, she finds herself utterly unmoved. In an untypical display of disdain, she dismisses his scribblings as formulaic pap. 'His hero and heroine had names, but needed them not, for they might just as well have been labelled hero and heroine.' As for his local colour, it 'consisted of the throwing in . . . of a few rustics speaking an unidentified dialect'. Laura thinks it 'a queer freak of human nature that one who knew and could appreciate all that was best in literature should fall to such a low level in his own writing'.

What ensures Laura's continuing friendship, despite her literary contempt, is the romantic story behind the Jeromes' marriage, which Laura finds 'as exciting as any novel'. Wilmot and Alicia had once lived close to each other, when she was a small girl and he was a medical student. He acted as an honorary uncle, playing games with her and even changing her nappies when necessary. But before she was two, Wilmot abandoned his medical studies and went to join in the Australian gold rush. He was last heard of in South Africa, prospecting for metals and tutoring the sons of a diamond merchant.

Meanwhile, by the time she was in her thirties, Alicia had become an orphan, and had backed out at the last minute from three engagements to be married. She had moved to Hampshire, resigned to a future of spinsterhood and dress-making, when Wilmot reappeared on the scene. He had returned to England, and had, with some difficulty, tracked Alicia down. He put up at a small inn, under the cover of being on a fishing holiday, and after some weeks they were married in secret, because the educational authorities at that time expected women teachers to resign from their positions on marriage. Their friendship with Laura apparently ends when she moves on at the end of the book, but the theme of the frustrated woman, imprisoned by circumstance and rescued by the arrival of a sensitive stranger, would recur in Flora's short stories in the 1920s.

Laura's closest relationship in Heatherley was also the most disruptive, and Flora's story of it has the frisson of thwarted romantic interest. One winter afternoon, a young man 'burst' into the Post Office (all Laura's encounters in the final version of *Heatherley* begin in this public trading place, where talking to strangers was perfectly in order). Richard Brownlow is a thick-set, ruddy-faced young man, with a small moustache and a shaggy overcoat, and Laura takes him for a farmer or game-keeper. In fact he worked in London for one of the big cable companies (placing him in a more sophisticated form of the same business as Laura), and is in the area visiting friends. He returns to Heatherley frequently, for weekends and holidays, and the two become good friends, discovering they have similar tastes and sense of humour. 'If one of the two began to quote poetry, the other capped the quotation, or held out a finger to link and called out the name of a poet to signify that their thoughts had been identical. And often the old childish proceeding did not end there, for the poet's name which first sprung to the lips of one would spring to the lips of the other. "Burns!" "Browning!" or "Keats!" they would cry simultaneously, and instead of linked fingers there were clasped hands and laughter.'

Richard's sister Mavis often accompanied him on his trips to
Heatherley. Mavis was also well read and fond of the countryside, but she was so exquisitely pretty, so 'dainty . . . and bird-like
in her movements', that she made even the petite Laura feel
clumsy. And she had an intellect which echoed her physique:
'she did not reason things out to a logical conclusion as Richard
did, but reached her conclusions by flashes of insight or by
wheeling and dipping in a kind of swallow flight'. Laura was
delighted by her new friends. They knew the latest catchwords,
the latest book releases and all the up and coming authors. Above
all, they were *modern*, truly *fin de siècle*, and Laura felt that at last
she had some companionship in which her slightly guilty desire
to be fashionable could be balanced out by serious conversation.

Mostly they liked to go for walks together, on dark nights
after the Post Office had closed, 'Mavis on Richard's arm on
one side, Laura on the other, chanting in unison the quatrains
of Omar Khayyám, or a chorus from Swinburne.' They fanta-
sized, parodied tragic writers and talked passionately about
Liberalism ('The miseries of the women chain-makers of
Cradley Heath, then much in the limelight, or those of the
sweated seamstresses of the East End of London, moved Richard
to wrath'). The expeditions sound so like the threesome night-
walks of Coleridge with Wordsworth and his sister Dorothy,
that Flora, when she came to re-imagine these evenings, may
have been guilty of a little plagiaristic ornamentation.

Despite this romantic intimacy, Laura does not reveal all her
secrets to her new friends. One, understandably, was the location of what she referred to as 'the heart of the wood', also *her*
heart, the kind of sequestered nook where she had always felt
she could be reflective and invisible and emotionally safe. It
was an 'oblong of lawn-like turf, threaded by a little stream . . .
shut in on every side by trees and thick undergrowth'. She

73

could 'steep herself' privately there, and 'think her own quiet thoughts'. But her public, fashionable, fantastical self was always up for some more playful melodrama. One night the three chums climb to the summit of a hill where a gibbet had once stood, and Laura, dropping to her knees, recites in 'trance-like tones an imaginary conversation between the two malefactors who she asked them to suppose had once suffered there, an effort which was applauded as worthy of Poe'.

Laura's account of an incident on one of these walks is a tantalizing passage. She takes Richard and Mavis to a remote part of the heath and shows them a patch of heather which, at a short distance, looks blighted and has a kind of reddish tinge. She takes them closer, and then, like a conjuror whipping away a handkerchief, reveals the true drama of what is happening. '[E]very individual plant was seen to be netted and dragged down to earth by the thin, red, threadlike runners of a parasite. They were horrified at the sight and asked the name of the plant with the stranglehold. Laura told them it was dodder and said that, if she were a novelist, she would write a book with that title. It would be the story of a man or woman – she thought a woman – of fine, sensitive nature, bound by some tie – probably marriage – to one of a nature which was strong, coarse, and encroaching, and would tell how, in time, the heather person shrank and withered, while the dodder one fattened and prospered.'

Richard and Mavis are pleased with Laura's conceit, despite its pessimistic theme, and, 'eating from a bag of cherries', they begin to discuss the plot, and the insensitivity of the dodder husband. Laura objects immediately to the casting of her newly created character as the villain of the piece: 'The dodder cannot help being dodder, it was made that way, and must act according to its nature, and in the same way, the dodder man has no evil intentions, he may even be kindly disposed; it just happens that his close proximity is ruinous. He thrives and becomes more and more bumptious, important, and respected – I think he must be a stockbroker, with a white waistcoat and a thick gold watch-chain – she – she painted quite good water-colours when a girl you know – she withers and shrinks into the mere wraith of a woman.'

Flora here is crediting Laura with a quite sophisticated understanding of ecology, and with resisting any sentimental temptation to attribute the power of choice to a plant (though she may not have known that dodder is not just a parasite but a botanical gypsy, a wandering organism with no attachment whatever to the ground). Her allegorical account of the nuances of one kind of marriage is simplistic (and later in her life Flora confessed that she always had problems in finding words for 'inner emotions'). But her description of the hus-band – the bumptious but respected businessman and his insignia of office – corresponds closely enough to the postal worker Flora was to marry in four years' time (see p. 87) that some commentators have assumed this is the adult Flora Thompson reflecting on her own marriage.*

* This may be so. Dodder is a rare plant now, but was common on the Surrey heathlands in the early twentieth century, though whether Flora invented her botanical parable at the time or half a century later is impos-sible to tell. But as a portrait of her own marriage it is, as we shall see, only half true, and is typical of the tangled problems presented by the dual time-frames in which Laura and Flora exist as narrators. Critics as diligent as Ruth Collette Hoffman have been caught out. Hoffman is a vigorous pro-ponent of reading Thompson as an imaginative storyteller and rejects the possibility of the dodder story referring to the Thompsons' marriage. 'Based on existing records, it appears that Thompson did not meet her future hus-band until she left Grayshott (the fictional Heatherley) in 1901' (endnote in *Without Education or Encouragement: The Literary Legacy of Flora Thomp-son*). But *Heatherley* was completed in 1944, forty-one years *after* the Thompsons' marriage.

What happens as the friendship between the three deepens has the scent of doom on it from the outset. The well-educated and worldly Brownlows decide to 'improve' Laura. They want her to move to London, their own permanent base. They prepare a tempting programme of visits to museums and galleries, and persuade her to prepare for a Civil Service examination, so that her career prospects could advance alongside her cultural enlightenment. Laura goes as far as to obtain a syllabus and pay a fee of one guinea to a Civil Service college so that she can begin taking a correspondence course. She knows in her heart that she isn't competitive enough for this kind of examination, and that she is lamentably deficient in essential disciplines like geography and arithmetic. But having paid her guinea, her 'peasant thrift' demands she perseveres, at least for a while. And when, for an essay on a recently read book, she chooses Henry James's *Portrait of a Lady*, she does at least earn a grudging compliment from her remote tutor: 'A curious choice. Don't care for James's work myself, but almost thou persuadest me!'

At least the trip to London turned out better. Laura had been to London before, but never after dark, and she is thrilled by the street smells ('orange-peel, horse-manure and wet clothes, with a dash of coal gas') and mêlée of people beneath the gas lamps. 'She fancied herself caught in a great sparkling net hanging amidst miles and miles of surrounding darkness.' They visit Richard and Mavis's mother, an ailing widow living in decaying elegance in south London, who is cordial towards Laura, but 'seemed to look on her as an intruder'. After she has gone to bed, they stay up like naughty children and listen to Richard reading salacious passages from copies of the notorious *Yellow Book* he'd picked up from a second-hand bookstall.

The next day, a Sunday, they take Laura on a trip around the

City, now empty of its thronging weekday workers. They visit Threadneedle Street, and gaze on the edifice of the Central Telegraph Office, known to Laura simply as 'T. S.' and 'figuring in her world as the centre of the universe'. They walk through Fleet Street and Johnson's Court, and pass 'without the faintest anticipatory thrill the office of the magazine whose editor would one day accept her first shyly-offered contribution' (Flora allowing Laura a brief prophetic glimpse of her own professional future.)

Laura loved the romance of the City, and like Richard Jefferies before her, glimpses a kind of beguiling wilderness in the labyrinth of ancient buildings and echoing passageways, 'where their footsteps rang loudly on the pavement and the sky, tinged with sunset, showed like a rose-coloured ribbon between the tall roofs.' But she quickly realizes that she could never live in London, that she needed the free air of the south country hills to survive. And back in Heatherley the next day, she writes to the secretary of the Civil Service College, cancelling her application, giving as an excuse that she had little chance of passing the exams, and had, in any case, a satisfactory post already. So ended, Flora concludes disingenuously, 'Laura's one bid for worldly advancement', knowing full well that she herself would make many more determined bids though other channels.

Laura never visited Richard and Mavis's London home again and, after this one visit, relations between the three began to cool. They still enjoyed gossiping and talking when the Brownlows paid their now occasional weekend visits to Heatherley, but 'a shadow, the shade of a shade had crept between them'. They were patently disappointed and hurt that Laura had rejected their plans for her improvement; and when she tried to explain her motives, she was told 'for the first time in her life, though not the last', that she cared more about places than people. Laura doesn't disagree, and tries to laugh their suggestion off by suggesting that she had been a cat in a previous existence, so of course she was territorial – a joke which simply offended them more.

The relationship finally collapses into melodrama, and Flora recounts its closing stages in high gothic style. One winter evening, just as she is closing up the Post Office, Laura spots Richard standing outside on the pavement. 'Against the dark background of the unlighted street, with the faint rays of the office oil-lamp falling upon it, his face looked unnaturally pale. His coat collar was turned up against the cold, which made him look hunched up and dejected.' She goes out to meet him, and he utters those fearful words 'I want to talk to you'. But there is no question of Laura taking him to her single room, with its provocative bed. So they walk out into the slush and fog. Richard has some bad news. Mavis has been ill, and has been diagnosed with the possible early signs of tuberculosis. She must go to France, or Bournemouth, or a sanatorium. But Richard isn't sure he can afford to pay for such expensive therapy.

Then, 'Pacing to and fro, enclosed in the fog, Richard opens his heart to Laura as never before.' And out comes a dismal and self-pitying tale – of the death of their father, the oppression of having to take financial responsibility for the family, his 'blubbering' whenever a bill arrived, his beloved sister's self-sacrificing labours scrubbing the scullery ... Then he blurts out 'And so it will always be with me. I can never marry, you know that, don't you Laura?' Laura's response is to 'stiffen inwardly', from, possibly, disappointment, or, more likely, surprise. Richard was too *flabby* a personality ever to have been romantically attractive to Laura, and 'Some mean little spirit said in her heart, "Good Heavens! surely he doesn't think I want him to marry me!"' But Flora allows Laura a more compassionate response: 'but another voice which was also her own told her it was no time for silly pride, and she said, as lightly as she was able, "But you don't want to marry anyone do you? And perhaps by the time you do, you'll have made a fortune."'

Still enveloped by fog, they hold hands to a soundtrack of water dripping from the boughs and the humming of telegraph wires. Richard agrees with Laura's supposition that they won't be seeing each other for some time. Before he disappears, without so much as a goodbye peck on the cheek, he intones into the dark: 'There will be no holidays for me, not even weekends, until Mavis is better.'

This proved to be true, and Laura and Richard met just once more, a year later. Meanwhile Mavis moves from one luxurious therapeutic resort to another. She sends postcards from Rome, a basket of spring flowers from the French Riviera. Her letters are so ebullient and affectionate that Laura begins to suspect her of malingering, 'petting' as she called it. Then the correspondence from both Richard and Mavis begins to peter out, and ceases altogether in 1903 (the year Flora gets married). But Laura remained grateful for their friendship, and 'the time she had spent in their company came to signify to her in retrospect the high-water mark of her youth.'

Towards the close of *Heatherley* Flora interjects a postscript to the Brownlow episode, which puts the fading of the relationship in a rather different light (though again attributes it to a now grown-up Laura): 'Many years after he and Mavis had passed out of her life, Laura's youngest son, then [in the 1930s] an engineering apprentice, passed to her over the supper-table one of his technical journals for her to look at the illustration of a new liner which had just been launched.' Turning the page, she was astonished to see a photograph of a very familiar face, balding and slightly plumper, with an account of the retirement of her one-time friend after a distinguished career with Cable & Wireless in the Far East.

The writer (and publisher of the full edition of *Heatherley*) John Owen Smith has found what is almost certainly this story in an edition of *The Zodiac*, Cable & Wireless's staff journal, for April 1937, describing the retirement of one William Burton Elwes, OBE. Many of the details about Elwes chime with Flora's account of Richard Brownlow – his physical description, the time spent in Hampshire, his love of books. Where they diverge is in the history of Elwes's family. His father, far from dying young and leaving them in penury, had been Archdeacon of Madras and had lived until 1924. And William's grandniece has told Smith that his sister Lilian never had tuberculosis, would never have considered doing anything as menial as working for a living, and was decidedly snobbish.

She also remembers 'Uncle Bill' as a bit of a flirt, and that he always had to get the approval of his sister before embarking on any serious relationship. If Richard Brownlow and William Elwes were the same man, it's conceivable that at the point his friendship with 'Laura' began to look serious, Lilian vetoed it, on the grounds of the latter's low social status. 'Mavis's' illness may well have been a fabrication, either by her brother to extricate himself, or by Flora, to save face.

But I'm doubtful whether there were any real romantic expectations on Flora's part, if the Richard Brownlow episode was indeed based on a real-life friendship. She is exceptionally evasive about her personal feelings in *Heatherley*, and if the relationship with 'Richard' had been a thwarted love affair, or if she had any inkling of deceit by 'Mavis', she would have excised the episode altogether. More probably Flora is remembering a real companionship and, forty years on, simply adding a few Grand Guignol touches. A suspicion of consumption in a story always added to its bohemian credentials.

★

Laura stays on in Heatherley for another year, but effectively vanishes as a person in Flora's recollections. After the departure of the Brownlows there are no mentions of new friends or adventures, nor any hint as to how Laura's hopes and dreams were evolving. The final chapters of *Heatherley* concentrate almost exclusively on the impact of world affairs on the village. The Boer War had started in 1899, and Flora's brother Edwin had enlisted immediately, aged just nineteen (Laura sees Edmund off at Aldershot station on 'a snowy Sunday morning'). But for a woman who has been building a picture of her young self as liberal and sensitive, Flora's description of the 'The Village in Wartime' is unsettlingly casual and detached – especially when you recall that Flora wrote these recollections after living through two more major wars, in the first of which her brother was killed, and in the second, her eldest son.

Her account of the patriotic hysteria that gripped rural Hampshire is, as you'd expect, vivid and sharp-eyed, a vision of national passion expressed through the physical. She describes the popular view of the Boers as wily, dirty, adulterous and addicted to brandy; and the intelligentsia's opinion that Britain needed a good war to stiffen the national sinews and reassert her world supremacy. Both views filtered down into behaviour in the village. Pro-Boers were ostracized, had their windows smashed and were burned in effigy. 'Tommy Atkins' (the Boer War version of 'Our Boys') was feted, and during march-pasts buoyed along by patriotic songs was given 'the addresses of complete strangers wishing to boast the distinction of receiving a letter from the Front'.

Tons of white enamel buttons with portraits of popular generals were sold in local shops to be worn as ornaments. The womenfolk made bandages and shirts, and in their leisure time indulged in the rage for displaying '[t]hat dashing new colour, the khaki of soldiers' field uniforms' in their coats and costumes.* Laura herself became a knitter, and started on a long scarf in bright red wool – provided, Laura stresses, not by herself, but by a charitable organization with more patriotic fervour than common sense. '[S]he had to repeat this many times to callers who had remarked that it would make a good mark "for one of these here snipers".'

Her observations are astute, and often blackly funny. She catches the countryside's view of the Boers as 'varmints', idiots from the next village, easily outsmarted by our home-grown yeomen. What is odd is the sense of her emotional detachment from what was happening, as if she were witnessing a rather unruly rural fete, not the penumbra of a three-year war in which 20,000 British men and an unknown number of Boers were killed. Laura seems unaware of, or reluctant to acknowledge, the British concentration camps that had been set up for Boer women and children, and which had been condemned by many of the feminist writers Flora had read, either at the time or in her later life.

* 'Military chic' – fatigues, 'camouflage' tights, metal belts, desert-toned headscarves – became fashionable on the catwalks again during the Afghanistan war *c.*2012.

It isn't that Laura is presented as a fence-sitter politically. She is largely in favour of the war, and sees her brother as 'a happy warrior', acting out for real the fantasies of romance and chivalry that had entranced them both as children. She is anxious about Edmund's fortunes, fighting on the veldt, but expresses no emotions whatsoever about the imperial fantasies that had sent him there. Perhaps this is Flora being a fastidious autobiographer. Perhaps, aged twenty-four, she was still 'Laura Looking On', observing the hubbub around her like a blasé or bewildered outsider, still unsure about where her commitments lay.

In the end, the *fin de siècle* moved on from being a style parameter and actually happened. One year later Queen Victoria died, which seemed in most people's eyes an even more significant event. Flora again avoids saying much about her own reactions, and gives instead a kind of profit-and-loss account of social change at the arrival of 'The New Century': the return of prosperity after the Boer War ended in 1902 alongside the spread of crime and disease in the mushrooming slums of the industrial cities; the rise of a new kind of celebrity culture in the press and in films, and of bland machine-made furniture – both evidence of the birth of mass consumption.

Flora (plainly writing now as an older woman looking back) confesses that she had had little personal experience of either extreme of the social scale. She was unashamedly one of the 'great middling mass' which, by and large, was benefiting from boons such as the old-age pension and tinned fruit 'brought from the ends of the earth to figure on the Sunday tea-table'. In the countryside, despite the continuing decline of the ancient peasant values of self-help and thrift, she saw plenty to hearten her: a less cloistered life for women, new village halls, cookery lectures, scholarships for village schoolchildren, and a rise in agricultural workers' basic wages, albeit just to fifteen shillings a week from their 1880s ground-base of ten shillings.

It is an even-handed summary, but again flat and dissociated. It is only when Flora describes the mourning of Queen Victoria through an account of the clothes people wore that the story comes alive again. The use of clothing was one of her life-skills, and became an increasingly sophisticated leitmotif in her writing. It is as if this constantly changing public membrane, this visible display by people of their social feelings, was easier for Flora to read than the mysterious world of their inner emotions at this convulsive time. Her account of the changing fashions following Victoria's death is a witty impressionist documentary, the shifting social landscape caught, as it were, by snapshots from the catwalk: 'Women of means ordered new all-black outfits; those whose means did not permit this expense ransacked their wardrobes for something black to wear, a less vain quest than it would be now . . . The very poor looked to their patrons for discarded black garments, or failing these, home-dyed their own clothes or sewed on to them bows of black crêpe . . . For the first three months after the death of the queen only the attire of the gipsies [of whom there were many still living on the heaths around Grayshott] provided a splash of colour in the gloom; then, as the days lengthened and brightened, black and white mixtures and soft tones of mauve and grey began to appear. Finally, women's dress that year went purple. Wine, plum, pansy, heather and lavender shades were in great demand. Traders sent their goods still in the piece and capable of taking such shades to the dye-vats, but a great stock of piece-goods, as well as made-up garments acquired before the general mourning, was left on their hands, and many of them went bankrupt.'

By the time Edward VII died in 1910, the whole paraphernalia of mourning had loosened up, along with the rest of society. Black kid gloves for men, all-enveloping black crêpe dresses for women, and mourning envelopes, so heavily bordered with black that the space left for the address was no bigger than a visiting card, had all become rarities.

In the end all this modernization made Flora's job extinct as well. Grayshott did not expand into a fashionable town as had once looked likely. Instead, Hindhead, a mile nearer to a railway station, became the commuters' location of choice. With the expansion in the population, a new Post and Telegraph Office was opened there in September 1900. The following day the number of telegrams sent and received by the Grayshott office slumped by 80 per cent. Flora was suddenly surplus to requirements and left for a Post Office job elsewhere later that year.

6. Writing as a Cottage Industry

Sometime around about 1901–1902, Flora Timms (as she then was) found a more down-to-earth and reliable companion than 'Richard Brownlow' and in the following year got married, when she was twenty-six years old. There are no records of where she lived and worked immediately after she left Grayshott, but she turns up in the 1901 census in Yateley, just north of Aldershot, working as a clerk in the local sub-Post Office. Post Office records show that her husband-to-be, John Thompson, also a postal worker, was in continuous employment at Bournemouth from 1891. However, in the same 1901 census, he is living in Aldershot, perhaps seconded there to help with the extra business generated by the Boer War (there was already an extensive army camp in the region), and this is probably where the couple met.

But they were married near London in January 1903, at the parish church of St Mary the Virgin in Twickenham, a location as seemingly random as many of Flora's other temporary roosts. There were no members of her family present, and no record of who gave her away. In a deleted section of the first draft of *Heatherley* Flora hints at a souring of the relationship between her and her father Albert: '[Laura] had not her former longing to go home, for her home was no longer what it had been. Her father's weakness for drink had grown upon him and, in consequence, relations between him and her mother were often far from amiable and though, before others, she still stood by him staunchly, hiding his faults and excusing his lapses, the old happy family atmosphere had gone.' Perhaps it was a reaction against her father's instability that caused Flora to settle down with such an unlikely partner as the stout, stolid and defiantly un-bohemian John Thompson, and to move with him to the suburbs of Bournemouth.

Thompson was two years older than Flora, and, by all accounts, a man of managerial authority and immaculate dress. There is a myth that he was oppressive and cruel towards Flora, and tried to deter her from writing. It's based on an assumption that the dodder story from *Heatherley* is a retrospective allegory of Flora's marriage, and on a casual, unsubstantiated phrase in Margaret Lane's biographical essay that Flora wrote 'secretly . . . because of her husband's disapproval'. But it was an idea which took root. In an introduction to a Folio Society edition of *Lark Rise* in 1979, Sir Hugh Casson quips that John 'seems to have been as dull as an unstamped envelope'. Even Ronald Blythe, reviewing Thompson's work in the same year, accepts this verdict uncritically. He describes her as a woman who 'was dragged into a prim suburban existence which she hated' by a husband who was 'embarrassed by her writing' and 'crushing in his attitude towards her'.

There is not much evidence to support this unflattering portrait of John's character; and it may be worth recalling that for the previous five years Flora had herself freely chosen a 'suburban existence' in Grayshott. John Owen Smith has tracked down several surviving ex-postal workers who remember John from the 1920s, when the couple were back living in north Hampshire, Flora had begun to have her work published and John had risen to the rank of postmaster. Louie Woods, a sorting clerk at the time, described him as a small and portly man, always smartly dressed in a newly pressed uniform and with the commanding presence of a sergeant-major. Gossip in the sorting office ceased when he entered the room.

Eileen Leggett, who worked in the same office as a telephonist, recalled him as 'very aloof and not popular among the postal staff; he was fair but very strict'. Her elder brother, who was a frequent customer, felt much the same. 'I recall how . . . I made my first withdrawal from my savings book, and with the patience of a schoolmaster, he handed me form after form until at last I made it out correctly and received the two shillings I'd applied for . . . His observation and supervision was somewhat irksome to the postal staff, but they had great respect for his fairness towards them and his devotion to the post office.' Eileen Leggett was a next-door neighbour of the couple in 1926 and saw no evidence that his fondness for order mutated into domination in the marriage. 'We knew nothing of her being a writer, but my mother, a keen judge of character, soon decided that Mrs Thompson was a "lady" but her husband "no gentleman". People think she was intimidated by him but, at least by the time I knew them, in her gentle way she managed him nicely.'

John may have been more overbearing twenty years previously, when writing was still no more than a pastime for Flora. And hints in the themes of her early stories – frustrated artistic women, the superiority of true friendship over marital obligation – suggest John may have been dull and inattentive. But the idea that he dominated Flora derives more from the stereotype of working-class women as passive and downtrodden, and of any gifts they might develop flowing from this suppression like juice from a squashed grape.

Nevertheless, John plainly felt his employment should take precedence, and the newly-weds set up house in Bournemouth, where he was already working as a sorting clerk and telegraphist. Flora couldn't join him, as the Post Office refused to employ married women. They rented a small house in Winton, a village lying just outside Bournemouth but being rapidly absorbed by it. Flora must have felt on familiar territory, for, like Juniper Hill, Winton had been established on common land that was enclosed in 1802, and was surrounded by a landscape of pine and birch and gorse-clad heath redolent of her talismanic country around Grayshott.

Such geographical synchronicities recur throughout Thompson's life, and a contemporary description of late nineteenth-century Winton in the parish magazine shows that the transitional character of the village, too, echoed that of Heatherley/Grayshott: 'Winton is neither country nor town, but seems to take practical hints from both . . . Some of its characteristics it may no longer retain. We mean the beauty of its golden flowers in May and its purple heather in August. Much of this wild natural beauty has already succumbed. But . . . it must be confessed that Winton's unique attraction consists not in these natural beauties which have their counterparts elsewhere, but in the affable style, disposition and arrangements of the working people's houses, such as in the newer parts of the settlement.'

Flora soon resumed her ramblings. She took to wandering the remnants of Winton heath, already being torn up by steam-driven traction-engines to make way for the advancing sprawl of Bournemouth. She had another favourite route over the county boundary into Dorset, towards Talbot Village. Talbot was a model village (another echo of the Surrey Hills), created in the 1860s by two philanthropic sisters. It had its own church, nineteen cottages in the Gothic style, each with an acre of garden, and a thriving school, with almost a hundred pupils by the time the Thompsons arrived. Its chief difference from any village Flora had experienced before was that the tenants of the cottages had to abide by strict codes of behaviour and decorum, a far cry from either Juniper Hill or Grayshott.

Flora's walks were soon cut short by the arrival of her first child, Winifred, in the autumn of 1903. She was, by her own confession, not a natural nurse, and her own children barely make an appearance in her writings, factual or fictional, except as minor impediments to her writing. It is a surprising omission for a writer who is so perceptive about her own youth and the child's imagination.

But she found compensations for the creative problems presented by the 'pram in the hall', as she recalled in a magazine article in 1921. 'With a house to run single-handed and with children being born and nursed my literary dreams faded for a time. But I still read a good deal. For the first time in my life I had access to a good public library,* and I slipped in like a duck slipping into water and read almost everything. I had no guidance except my own natural taste. But perhaps I was fortunate in this, as I was able to follow my own bent.'

If that suggests the random browsing of an enthusiastic armchair reader, Flora's breakdown of the contents of her reading programme is more like the syllabus of a rigorous extra-mural degree course: 'I went right back to the beginning, read the Greeks and Romans in translations; read the English poets; the English Novelists; the English Critics; nibbled at translations of the French writers; even tried my teeth upon philosophy and mysticism! Read Ibsen, Shaw, Yeats, and all the Celts. Became enamoured of the new poetry, at least of the work of those poets who passed as new in pre-war time.'

Flora may have been over-egging her literary foraging for the sake of her newly acquired public (she had had her first book of verse published that year aged forty-four), and the clipped journalistic phrasing is not really her style. But her

* Bournemouth public library opened in 1893, and was only the second in England to allow readers open access to the bookshelves.

writing in the 1920s and 30s backs up a formidable history of reading. And between the strictly literary classics, she was reading avidly in the fields of evolutionary biology, botany and rural history.

Did she also find time to *write*, in those earlier years in Bournemouth between 1903 and 1914? Almost certainly, at least in her head, as she ruminated on the techniques of her role models. And most probably on paper too, in an informal and exploratory way. But she was finding the responsibilities of bringing up a family on John's 'pitiful' wages (she makes no mention of any domestic help) straining on her nerves and energy. Her second child, Henry Basil, was born in October 1909, and the family moved to a slightly larger house two streets away, which Flora promptly renamed after her beloved Grayshott.

Yet her literary dreams had only temporarily faded. In 1910 she began taking the *Lady's Companion* ('A Home Journal for Women and Girls' founded in 1900), a rather earnest weekly magazine aimed at the female middle classes, which carried short stories and articles on self-improvement. It had a column entitled 'Our Book Club', written by the pseudonymous 'Dorothea', which encouraged readers to tackle contemporary English novelists such as Chesterton, Kipling and Belloc. Allied to this was a regular competition (also judged by Dorothea) in which readers were invited to submit 300-word essays. Essay contests were popular in the better class of periodicals of the time and provided an entrée into the literary world – as one modern historian patronizingly put it – for 'slum children with some writing talent'.

Early in 1911, the competition subject was the work of Jane Austen. Austen was one of Flora's favourite authors, and she decided to try her chances, and expose herself to that public judgement she had always feared. The need to bring in more money for her family to supplement her husband's meagre wages was an incentive, too. The supposedly disapproving John Thompson was at least not blind to this possible benefit from his wife's scribbling. The magazine insisted on entries being typewritten, and he either bought Flora a typewriter or lent her his own (he was a trade union secretary at the time). Flora accordingly typed up her measured tribute, and won. She was thirty-four years old and the mother of two children and, at long last, had a piece of work published, in the *Lady's Companion* of 25 February 1911.

Her piece was a sound enough summary of Austen's achievements and standard critical appreciations, and might have merited a B-plus as an undergraduate essay. She notes, with approval, how Austen had departed from the contemporary conventions of 'involved plot, sensational incident, and the long arm of coincidence' and wrote 'quiet, gentle stories . . . dealing with everyday people and events'; and how (one senses a nod of sympathy here, too) 'the public did not immediately recognise her genius or appreciate the gentle sarcasm that plays around her characters'.

Flora was galvanized by her victory. For the rest of 1911 she devoted most of the time, when she wasn't looking after a house and family, to writing entries for the *Lady's Companion* contests. In April she won second prize for an essay on Emily Brontë, which was also published in the magazine. Later the same month she received an honourable mention for her essay on 'Queen Katharine of Aragon', and later in the year, for her meditations on Thackeray and on 'Poetry versus Prose'. In July she won first prize again. The subject was Shakespeare's heroines and Flora chose Juliet. Her opening paragraph showed that she still had her childhood fondness for over-perfumed landscape description, to which had been added a willingness to please her readers with comforting clichés. 'The very name of Juliet calls up a vision of the Capulets' garden in old Verona, of those glimmering midsummer nights, when the wandering wind came laden with the heavy perfume of jessamine and tuberose and the nightingale sang all night in Juliet's pomegranate tree.' Stark accounts of pig-killing in the winter mud of Oxfordshire seem a very long way away.

Feeling well settled in the bosom of the *Lady's Companion*, she made a bold move early in 1912, and submitted her first short story, 'The Toft Cup', the first of five which would appear in the magazine before it folded in 1915. Short fiction had been a mainstay of women's magazines since the mid nineteenth century and had begun to conform to a fairly standard protocol. Stories would focus on the trials and rewards of love and marriage. Sexuality might be flirted with, but never explicitly explored. A sentimental tone was conventionally a *sine qua non* for readers, but an excess of philosophical reflection was to be avoided – unless it helped justify a less-than-happy ending.

Flora's *Lady's Companion* stories satisfied all these criteria, and some of her own. They featured strong, often thwarted heroines, who are rescued or redeemed by sensitive, bookish men. They have rural settings in or near the New Forest, the closest expanse of wild country to Bournemouth (Flora went there for outings by train, sometimes with her children). 'The Toft Cup' was published in January 1912. It features a young woman, Grace Coombe, on the point of having to sell her family's old farm in the Forest, following the death of her parents. There's no money coming in to pay the rent, and she is resigned to taking work as a housemaid and packing her granny off to live in a small cottage on her old-age pension. An auctioneer arrives to make an inventory for the sale, the young, blue-eyed

Edmund Varney. He gazes at Grace – and her at late father's generous collection of books – with almost equal longing. 'Everything in this room is for sale except the books,' Grace points out. 'I feel I could never part with them.' 'Ah,' Edmund enquires, 'you love them for your father's sake?' 'For my father's sake, and their own – or, perhaps, I should say, *my* own sake,' Grace replies, and, using the nickname that Laura was given in Candleford, explains that she is 'a real bookworm'.

Of course, Edmund is as well, and the couple sit in the parlour as the winter sun sets, discussing literature and Edmund's other job as a reporter on the *Christminster Herald*,* and the column he was contributing to *Simple Life Magazine* on forest lore. Ferreting about later, Edmund discovers a seventeenth-century earthenware loving-cup at the back of a cupboard, a rare example of the work of one Thomas Toft. After more of this kind of reader-pleasing coincidence, he sells the Toft Cup for a considerable sum to the local museum. The farm is saved, Edmund and Grace fall in love, and Granny is invited to take up residence with them. But not before she has 'told the bees' what was happening – a widespread rural custom that decreed that the house bees must be the first to be informed of major domestic events. It was Flora's first account of a tradition that she was to progressively elaborate in her journalism until it became one of the set-pieces in *Lark Rise*.

Many of the features of 'The Toft Cup' recur in the other *Lady's Companion* stories. In 'Nut Brown Maiden' (September 1912), a young artist sketching in the New Forest falls in love

* Christminster is the name Thompson uses for the local market town in all her New Forest stories. It also happens to be the pseudonym Thomas Hardy used for Oxford, a long way to the north. It's conceivable that Thompson hadn't read Hardy by 1912, though she was familiar with and wrote about his work ten years later.

with and proposes to a gypsy girl, despite the gap in their social status. (Flora also tries a more extensive rendering of rural dialect here, something she had experimented with in 'The Toft Cup'.) 'His Lady of the Lilac' (May 1914) features another journalist, Philip Allington, who writes 'Nature Notes' and casual contributions to magazines. He inherits a derelict mansion and falls in love with the girl-next-door, a deep-feeling and well-read doctor's daughter. 'They found a wonderful affinity in their tastes and ideals. Philip's favourite books always turned out to be Esther's favourites, too. He had been alone in the world so long that it was a continual wonder to him to share his thoughts with another.'

To what degree these stories expressed an unfulfilled romantic streak in Flora is hard to say. Their predominant characters – women fallen on hard times, sensitive men, aspiring writers – appear too often to be purely coincidental. But then these were stock characters in the popular fiction of the early twentieth century, who would have appealed to large numbers of housebound women. In *Lark Rise* Flora describes the typical themes of stories in magazines such as the *Family Herald*, *Tit-Bits* and *Bow Bells*: 'a romantic love story, in which the poor governess always married the duke, or the lady of title the gamekeeper'. In her own fiction she was expressing the female *Zeitgeist* as well as her own frustrations.

But in 1912 she formed a liaison that suggests a degree of at least intellectual neediness, and which was to have an impact on her professional future. In her search for ways of making money from her writing, Flora was continuing to write essays as well as stories. In the spring of 1912 the *Literary Monthly* published an ode on the sinking of the *Titanic* by the Scots poet Ronald Campbell Macfie, and alongside it ran a competition for readers, inviting them to submit their critiques of the poem.

The ode was florid and excruciating, echoing the doggerel of Macfie's fellow countryman William McGonagall, but couched in hyperventilating phraseology. The poem begins:

> O, ribbed and riveted with iron and steel,
> Cuirassed and byrnied, breathing smoke and flame,
> Cleaving the billows with her monstrous keel,
> A Titan challenging the gods she came!
> The surf piled lilies round her eager prow,
> The wind made music through her mighty spars,
> Her hot heart thudded, thundered, and her brow
> Had converse with the stars.

It's hard to imagine what Flora admired in the poem. But she was already worldly enough as a writer to realize that commenting on a still-fresh national tragedy was a good career move. That she won isn't remarkable, as she could already produce the kind of material that judges and the general public wanted to read. What is curious is that she was able to find and express so much of value in the work that Macfie, perhaps lacking more public plaudits, wrote to her personally to express his appreciation, and later came to visit her, unannounced, in Bournemouth. He went on to become a mentor to Flora, the first professional writer to take any interest in her literary ambitions.

'Macfie was a supporter of causes,' Flora's biographer Gillian Lindsay has written, 'and Flora became one of his causes.' His influence was a mixed blessing. Flora needed encouragement and some kind of umbilical link to the world of writing. She was accomplished enough not to be smothered by the miasma of Macfie's style, but didn't have sufficient confidence to know when she was being given bad advice about her future direction. More to the point, she had a crush on him.

Macfie was eleven years older than Flora, and had qualified as a physician in Aberdeen in 1897. He was also an eccentric polymath who would have rubbed along well with the Surrey Hilltops set, being an ardent follower of a multitude of 'isms', regardless of their mutual incompatibility. He was a Liberal Member of Parliament, a poet and children's story-writer, an evangelical vegetarian, a vitalist* who rejected Darwin's theory of evolution, and a pacifist who, during the Great War, published a bizarre and disturbing eugenic argument about the biological benefits of warfare. Male deaths during the war, he suggested, created a surplus of women, and 'nature has wisely arranged' that the surviving young men were attracted by women with 'characteristics that imply a superior capacity for motherhood . . . [thus] every war will do something to set up evolutionary tendencies opposite to its own, brutal, truculent, anti-social spirit'. It may have been the vitalist message in Macfie's Titanic ode (he basically laments the tragedy, but sees some deep evolutionary purpose in it) that first attracted Thompson's praise.

Photographs show Macfie as craggily handsome, with rather dangerous eyes. Flora may have been physically attracted to him, but would never have admitted it. What drew her were his artistic stature and that unfailing aphrodisiac, flattery. He fitted the role of the experienced older man, a figure she had responded to before. Like 'Mr Foreshaw' in *Heatherley* (but

* Vitalism is a doctrine which originated in classical times, and has at its heart a belief in 'life energy', some indefinable force that is inherent in all living and organic things but absent from the inorganic. The doctrine was teetering into disrepute in the early twentieth century, as scientists uncovered more and more about the mechanical workings of animate bodies and began synthesizing organic compounds from inorganic chemicals. Today, ironically, as systems theory and epigenetics show living things to be vastly more complex than the sum of their parts, biologists take a more kindly view of the spirit of vitalism.

unlike her husband), Macfie had travelled widely, meditated deeply, was intimate with the famous and the high-born. He knew and had collaborated with the poet and children's author Lady Margaret Sackville (a relative of the Sackville-Wests), a relationship which was to have contrasting effects on Thompson's legacy.

The correspondence and occasional meetings between Macfie and Flora continued until his death in 1931. Some of his letters survive, and their encouraging and lofty tone must have been a tonic to Flora, a blessing sent down from the gods. When she reached her fortieth birthday, Macfie wrote: 'Forty! what is forty? I am fifty-one; but if I could yet have ten years of opportunity to write I should be content. Look forward! Rejoice in your great gift and fight for opportunity, even if it be ten years later; and perhaps I who am still fighting may in a few years be able to find some ways and means for you. Who knows?' Flora reciprocated, and did strive for opportunities. Five years later, at Macfie's instigation, she put together a slim volume of her poetry (*Bog-Myrtle and Peat*, see below) and dedicated it to him, along with one of the verses. It is a hymn to an Olympian:

> Yours are the moors, the billowy seas,
> Tall mountains and blue distances.
> Mine is a cottage garden, set
> With marigold and mignonette,
> And all the wildling things that dare,
> Without a fostering gardener's care.
> Yet very well-content I rest
> In my obscure, sequestered nest;
> For from my cottage garden I
> Can see your cloud-peaks pierce the sky!

But Flora's everyday letters to Macfie have not survived. When Margaret Lane was researching her early essay on Thompson's life in the late 1940s, she wrote to Lady Margaret Sackville to enquire about them, under the impression that Sackville was Macfie's executor. Sackville's response was robust and dismissive, and was documented by Lane years later: 'It is sad, therefore, that her letters, many of which he had kept, were destroyed after his death by his literary executor, Lady Margaret Sackville. Macfie was an attractive man, particularly to aspiring literary ladies, and Margaret Sackville, who had collaborated with him in two small volumes of fairy tales, presumably resented this "warm and grateful friendship", as he described it on the fly-leaf of a book he was presenting to his "poet-friend Flora Thompson". There seems to be no other explanation of her destruction of the letters. She "saw no point", she replied to my enquiry about them many years ago, "in keeping such rubbish", and had consequently burned them.'

A less fanciful explanation might be that the letters were indeed little more than stilted fan-mail. But the story of their loss may be less straightforward than either of these possibilities. Margaret Lane was wrong in her assumption that Margaret Sackville was Macfie's executor. In 1919 he made a will in which he bequeathed his small estate to a Rose Mildred Sleeman, whom he described as 'an intimate friend'. He also made her his literary executor. What his letters were doing in the possession of another woman, who moreover felt she had the right to burn them, is a mystery known only to Macfie's Muses.

7. The Journalist: forest fantasies

In the years before the Great War, Flora freelanced for several journals, including the socialist *Daily Citizen*. In 1913 she sold a story called 'The Leper' to the *Literary Monthly*, the journal which had published Macfie's *The Titanic (an Ode of Immortality)*. Perhaps the great man had interceded on her behalf; it was a considerable step up for Flora to have a story in a literary monthly after working for the women's weeklies. 'The Leper' was also a different kind of story, a historical romance set in the Middle Ages. It's a tale about a young husband who contracts leprosy and is banished to a monkish cell in the woods, and is told by Flora in the fashionable 'Celtic Twilight' style. But if the style and subject were a departure, Flora stuck to her home turf. The story is set on the Isle of Wight, a short boat journey from Bournemouth.

The following August the war began. The Thompsons weren't immediately affected. John, then thirty-nine, wasn't expected to fight, and felt secure enough to move the family again, to a slightly bigger detached house nearby – which, like the previous one, was promptly renamed Grayshott Cottage. But as the losses in the trenches mounted and Zeppelin raids brought the war into Britain's own backyard, the bullish mood of late 1914 – 'It will all be over by Christmas' – began to fade. Escapist romance didn't fit the national mood, and the *Lady's Companion* folded early in 1915. Flora consequently lost her main source of income from writing, and began sending stories, poems and feature articles to other publications. She had little success, and it was as much out of a personal sense of frustration as any strong political commitment that she became a regular attendee at suffragette gatherings in Bournemouth. Then, in April 1916, Flora heard that her brother Edwin had been killed in action in Belgium. He had been at the Front for only three weeks, and died with a copy of Sir Walter Scott's poems in his pocket.

Flora's daughter Winifred, then twelve years old, remembers her mother being heartbroken, simply stopped in her tracks; and it may have been consideration for his wife as much as his own hopes of self-improvement that persuaded John to look for a new start for the family. Two months after Edwin's death, he applied for a job which had been advertised in the *Post Office Circular*. It was for a salaried sub-postmaster's position, a considerable rise in status for him. But it was the location of the Post Office that was more significant. It was at Liphook in Hampshire – a small town just three miles from Flora's Grayshott, and the heathy hills she had loved so much. John got the job, and in August 1916 moved Flora back to Hampshire, a gesture which doesn't quite fit with the conventional image of him as an inveterate emotional bully, indifferent to his wife's feelings and ambitions.

The post-house in Liphook was a gaunt, two-storey terrace next door to the Post Office, and bore the euphemistic name 'Ruskin House'. It must have been in need of serious renovation, as the Post Office spent over a hundred pounds making it habitable for the Thompsons. One bonus from this was that Flora could now have her own writing room, from which the children were barred. But she had little time to spare for writing in these mid-war years. The Post Office was deluged with incoming mail for the big army camp on Bramshott Common, and she decided that her best contribution to the war effort would be to go back to her old job. She got up at four in the morning to sort the mail before getting the children ready for school. During the day, young Canadian troops destined for the front line would march past the Post Office on their way to the station, a constant reminder of her lost brother. Her husband often slept at the office on a camp bed close to the telegraph machine, ready to take urgent messages.

Then Flora became pregnant again. It would be easy to assume that, nine years after Winifred's birth, this was an unplanned surprise. But Flora conceived the child just eight months after her brother's death, and may have been grasping for something to fill the gap he had left in her heart. Whatever lay behind it, a pregnancy in the middle of a war was a taxing prospect. There were no old baby clothes to recycle, as there had been in Juniper Hill. Fuel was desperately short and the price of coal had risen so sharply that housewives were saving clinker to burn. Sugar, butter and meat were strictly rationed. By a stroke of fortune, when Flora's third child Peter Redmond was born in October 1918, the war was about to end, but its fall-out was far from over, even in rural Hampshire. The influenza pandemic which swept across Europe that winter hit Liphook hard. More than 300 of the Canadian soldiers who had just returned to their local barracks died of the disease, and are buried, surrounded by maple trees, in the small parish churchyard. Then Flora's husband and her two eldest children were struck down. She had to keep three fires going in three different rooms, as well as cope with a three-month-old infant and John's temporary replacement at the Post Office, who was billeted with them. 'I don't know how I did it,' she wrote to a friend later. 'When I weighed myself afterwards I had gone down to seven stone.'

Indomitability was a necessity in the aftermath of the Great

War. There was mass unemployment amongst demobbed soldiers and a rising sense of disgruntlement amongst women. During the war they had been valued as industrial workers and had experienced a taste of independence and respect. Now they were being told to go back to the kitchen. Flora's response was to go back to her writing room. Time was suddenly not a problem. She was no longer needed to sort wartime mail, and Winifred and Henry were both settled in private day-schools in the area. But after five years in which she'd written little and published nothing, she was short of practice and low in confidence. So perhaps it is no surprise that her first tentative attempts to begin again don't directly tackle the war which had had such an overwhelming impact on her personal and social life. But two unpublished stories which almost certainly date from this time are touched with melancholy and disappointment. And they are composed in two contrasting styles, as if she were using them as literary litmus papers.

'The Awakening' is unlike anything else Flora wrote. It is a melodramatic tragedy, about an impoverished woman writer who has taken to the streets and is 'rescued' by a rich benefactor, who takes her as his mistress. On a brief return to her room, en route to a mock honeymoon in the warm south, she discovers a letter from a publisher, informing her that she has won a prize and had her novel accepted, and enclosing a cheque for £400. In a fit of self-disgust at what she has allowed herself to become, she tears up the cheque and her kept-woman's allowance, and throws herself out of the window. The story's subject matter was probably too adult for Flora's usual magazine outlets, even by broadened post-war standards. But Flora goes further, and tries for a style which is not only sophisticated, but borders on the decadent. The story is set in London and begins with a night-time pick-up in a taxi. Despite her supposed poverty, the gorgeous red-head is clad in a 'stylish mauve travelling dress' when her benefactor takes her back to his bachelor flat and 'the inevitable happened'. (Mauve is described as 'the colour of her name-flower', though her name is never mentioned. It was also, of course, Flora's iconic shade.)

One evening, 'wrapped in a Mandarin's gown of yellow satin, the spoil of his travels', she gets up from the sofa and explores the apartment, and discovers her benefactor's books, books that she knew of! They talk the night away, about art and literature and men and travel. The man is, at heart, a classic Flora hero, scarred only by the existential opportunities offered by chance and the city. On their ill-fated escape to the sun, he begins to worry about why she is taking so long in her lodgings. He rushes up to the room, and at the open window becomes aware of a commotion in the street below. He sees a crowd which has gathered 'round a fluttering heap of white and mauve'; and the story ends with his 'frenzied cry', 'My wife! My wife!'

'The Glimpse' also ends with a woman surrendering to disappointment, but in less sensational circumstances. Nora Kayman is a stock Flora character, an elementary school-teacher who has come to regard her life as pedestrian and unfulfilling, and the story has many echoes of Flora's own experiences as a wife and mother shunted about hither and thither. After 'sixteen years in Manchester' (the same length of time Flora had been married to the civic-minded John), Nora's husband moves her and their children down to 'Verwood' (an invented New Forest place-name used elsewhere by Thompson), where he's been offered a post as a headmaster. Nora is affronted that she wasn't consulted about the move, but looks forward to a life less constrained by childcare and the proximity of the in-laws, and the necessity of always just 'making ends meet'. She takes advantage of her new rural surroundings by devoting herself to landscape-painting on the heath and one day is approached by a man, 'older . . . with crisped grey-sprinkled hair, and rugged features', who turns out to be a 'world-famous' artist. He tells her that she 'cannot draw . . . but you have genius – the poetry of the thing', and he offers to give her lessons while he is staying in the region. She considers his offer (there is an intriguing Freudian slip here in Flora's uncorrected typescript: 'He meant to help her. To give her a good tome'), but on returning finds her husband George agog with news. He has found her an official paid post as the headmaster's wife – and has persuaded his mother to move in indefinitely to help care for the children. 'Fate, in the shape of podgy George Kay-man, had swung back the gold gates again, and it was but a glimpse poor, enslaved Nora had caught.'

Flora seems to have been in a similar mood to Nora. At the bottom of her typescript, submitted to and rejected by an unnamed periodical, there is a scrawled note in pencil: 'I'm sorry to send this crude undeveloped thing but no time or heart to re-write it.'

★

Sometime during 1919, aware that she was no longer producing marketable material, Flora responded to an advertisement in the *Daily News*, which was offering postal writing courses from the Practical Correspondence College in London. There is no record of how long she signed up for, or what kind of material she submitted. But it earned her fulsome praise from one of the tutors, A. Brodie Frazer, a staff writer on the *Daily News*. She kept his response as a memento amongst her papers: 'This is really good. You have handled the situation with the mastery of genius. Please send to one of the magazines on the list. I am proud of this story; it does you the highest credit.'

One of the magazines he may have recommended was *The Catholic Fireside*, as Flora almost immediately submitted to its editor a slightly reworked version of her story 'The Leper', which had already appeared in the *Literary Monthly* seven years previously. The magazine published it in January 1920, and Flora sold six more stories to them that year. They are still sentimental in tone and predictable in plot, but have a distinctly post-war edge and reveal a growing political awareness on Flora's part. Her stock characters are still there, but they are moving in a changing social landscape, in which there is now a 'new poor' as well as a new class of *arrivistes*, many of whom had amassed their fortunes during the war. 'The Hermit's Yew' explores the collision between traditional values and what Flora calls 'profiteering', via the felling of an ancient village yew by an entrepreneurial incomer. 'The Profiteers' is set in a smart country hotel, where the old aristocracy and the new lower middle classes glare daggers at each other over the perfectly laid dining tables. Into their midst strides a classic Thompson hero, a young doctor with 'the eyes of a poet and dreamer'. Allan Neal is also a class migrant, having devoted his life to treating the poor, and he cuts through the stand-off by falling for the daughter of a philanthropic industrialist (he made his money from wartime condensed milk), who is also staying at the hotel. There are doctors and journalists in most of these post-war stories. There are also determined autodidacts, whose talents overcome their educational and social shortcomings. The hero of 'The Uphill Way', Dr Carstairs, is all of these things and eventually finds fulfilment when his enthusiasm for amateur astronomy lands him a column called 'The Sidereal Heavens'. 'Our Contemporary' features a woman editor of a family provincial newspaper, which is driven into near-collapse by the arrival of a new mass-circulation title, owned by a wealthy, Oxford-educated outsider. Flora and 1920s magazines being what they were, the clash is averted by a comprehensive merger, the combination of both titles into 'one really first-class paper'. 'But this was only the prelude,' runs the story's closing sentence, 'the real romance came later!'

Flora's late stories are somewhat redeemed because they feature clashes of social manners as well as values, and this was her strength. But privately she was dreaming of a different kind of writing from family dramas with obligatory happy endings, and from the 'sugared love-stories' which had been the livelihood of her doomed authoress in 'The Awakening'. And here she was fortunate in having a foothold in *The Catholic Fireside*. It was a middlebrow magazine aimed at 'Catholic womanhood' and, as well as short fiction and poetry, carried features on fashion, cookery, gardening and 'women's interests'. E. Nesbit, co-founder of the Fabian Society and author of the classic *The Railway Children*, was a regular contributor in the 1920s. Flora never converted to Catholicism (though throughout her life she was attracted by the extravagant details of its rituals, and her stories are dotted with subtle Catholic references and tracklements). But she admired the magazine's feminist and radical edge, and later in 1920 put to the editor an idea for a series of monthly nature notes. From many hints in her stories – male characters who were also nature columnists, landscape settings painted with a meticulous attention to ecological detail – she had been longing to write along these lines for at least seven years.

The editor of *The Catholic Fireside* liked Flora's suggestion, and the first 'Out of Doors' column appeared in January 1921. Her February column starts boldly and economically. We're in the present, and in, we presume, Flora's real world: 'All day yesterday it rained. Not the fine, icy rain of a month ago, but great, warm, plashing drops, putting new life into grass and herbage and washing away the last hill-top and hedge-row remnant of the snow.' That morning she had been to 'Forestmere' (probably Bournemouth, though the real Forest Mere is a tiny settlement west of Liphook) 'in search of a washer woman'. Then she takes off, plunges down forest tracks, glimpses wild geese and feral snowdrops on the shore of a lake and, back in the town, watches a seaside Punch and Judy show.

The writing teeters on quaintness too often to be successful ('Master Rat' makes an appearance, as does 'Mother Earth turn[ing] in her sleep'). But more disorientating is the fact that we're increasingly not sure where we are. The piece starts in the New Forest and ends there, as Flora returns from her seaside outing, which, from Bournemouth, would have involved a cross-country hike of ten miles. It turns out this is where she 'lives'. The 'Forestry Corps' have felled a big cedar by her house and, as she goes indoors, she fills 'the loose wide pockets of my coat – the coat I love so for its Franciscan colour and texture – with the chips. They are burning on the hearth now, filling my cottage room with richest fragrance. This is no fire to work by. A sewing machine would be an anomaly! Nor will I open the library parcel, although I have just brought it in from the woodshed, where the postman had left it. I will take down "Urn Burial", or shall it be my Cranshaw?'

This sensuous, aesthetic fantasy has some significance. In reality the author was living in a drab terraced house in Liphook High Street, forty miles north of the New Forest. She was married and looking after three children. Against every convention of 'Nature Note' writing, Flora had begun from the outset to create a fictional persona for herself. Over the months that followed she elaborated as freely on the life and character of this retiring bluestocking, who was comfortable settling down alone for the evening with Sir Thomas Browne, as she did on the Hampshire countryside.

It wasn't as if she needed these diversions into a fantasy life to generate material for her copy. According to local reports, she was walking up to twenty miles a day after finishing her domestic chores, over a landscape vaster and more complex than anything she had experienced before. Her new literary parish had many of the same ingredients – heathland, pine-wood, acid bog – as her old Grayshott stamping ground, but to the north and west it took in the steep hills of the Hampshire weald, with their hanging beechwoods and downland, the whole making up a mosaic of wild country that stretched almost unbroken to the New Forest. Joe Leggett, who spent his childhood in the adjacent hamlet of Griggs Green (and from 1926 was her next-door neighbour there), remembers meeting Flora out on her rambles: 'She was a familiar figure to me, who always seemed to appear in the remotest parts of Woolmer Forest, Weavers Down, Bramshott Common, out towards Milland and around Waggoners Wells or Forest Mere. She often spoke to me as I roamed the wilderness looking for birds' nests. She had a kind authoritative voice imploring me not to disturb or rob the nests . . . The people of Liphook were unable to arrive at a solution as to what made her walk the numerous paths, to stand gazing at whatever caught her eye, a bird in flight, foxes in an open space enjoying a gambol in the sun, a fallen tree or a farmer ploughing a field.'

Back in *The Catholic Fireside*, the columnist's year moved forward. Spring has arrived on the hills, and Flora declaims on the wild flowers. The blackthorn 'flung a handful of snowy petals upon the rough plank covering' of an abandoned well at the military camp. The wood anemone is 'the frail, wan, shivering wind-flower of the Greeks'. She picks basketfuls of primroses (but they are for 'the Bermondsey school-children') and then bluebells, but she 'must not call them bluebells . . . Last year Fiona would not hear of it; that name was sacred to the bonny bluebells of her own beloved Scotland'.

Fiona is an actress from London, and makes her first appearance in the column in April, when Flora recalls her visit the previous year: 'I have a vision of her now, racing between wet sweetbriar hedges, her green smock billowing, April incarnate; or practising her dance steps beneath the orchard trees, flinging short, bright locks back from eyes the colour of dim, distant hills, as she looked up to throw a smile and a kiss to me at the bedroom window.' The almost Sapphic abandon of this description is the more remarkable when you realize that Fiona is entirely a creature of Flora's imagination.

The sophisticated identity Flora is striving to create for herself often overwhelms her prose. Hampshire is likened to a 'dark Madonna, with heather-purple robe and deep pinetresses'; and 'Spring, in all the glory of her festal robes, is regnant', she writes in May – just before another fantasy figure, 'Father Conlan from Boldrewood' (Boldre is a real New Forest village), comes over for tea, and teases her for not knowing the nurseryman's names for her old roses. The following month Father Conlan is revealed to be writing a biography of Francis of Assisi, which Flora finds insensitive to the 'mean and ugly' quality of real poverty. The good Father has sold his tulip bulbs to raise money for starving Russian children, and practises 'spiritual poverty' by giving up sugar. To which Flora responds by bringing out brown bread for tea, but 'no butter, for I too would be a humble follower of St Francis and his lovely lady, call her Poverty or Simplicity, whichever you will'. Later she name-drops spring poems – Shelley's 'Skylark', Keats's 'Night-ingale', Hardy's 'Thrush' – and has a reverie about outdoor reading: 'I carry abroad . . . old, quiet, soothing things – "The Excursion", "The Faery Queen", and an old battered, dog-eared book of sonnets, of which the chief merit is that it exactly fits the pocket of my knitted coat.'

At this point the descriptions of the manners and accoutre-ments of the journalistic aesthete are so wickedly sharp that it is possible that Flora was deliberately parodying the charged rural romanticism that was currently in vogue. Mary Webb's novels of rustic life, with their gothic atmosphere and mor-bidly overstated prose, had begun to appear in 1916, and would get their come-uppance in Stella Gibbons's lampoon *Cold Comfort Farm* in 1932. But their counterpart, the sometimes self-righteous prose of the back-to-the-land intelligentsia, had so far remained unscathed. Nothing in Flora's personality or in her off-the-page life suggests she had the confidence to poke fun at literary high fashion, or for that matter to mock (rather than scold) her own fancifulness. But she did have the courage to break with literary convention, and 'Out of Doors', with its whiffs of satire and unashamed blending of documentary and fantasy, might be regarded as a rather bold experiment in mod-ernism were it not such a blatant exercise in wish-fulfilment.

By the summer of 1921, the dream-life of the reclusive author has become the dominant theme in the column. In June, directly following what are presumably real observations on the domestic affairs of a family of red squirrels, Flora launches into an exact description of her imaginary New Forest cottage. 'The lane which leads from my house to the highway is one cool tunnel of greenery; even the light which filters through is tinged with green. The garden is overgrown and overflowing.

I always lose control of it about this time of year. Honeysuckle and crimson-rambler ramp about the porch and eaves; to look at the cottage, one would think that none but happy days could come to those whose pleasant lines were cast there. Not so! Tragedy once made it her abode. Some day I must tell you the story, but not in this glowing June weather; it is a tale for a winter night.'

Flora never gets round to telling this story in full, but hints that it concerns a 'famous woman writer who lived in the cottage for a few months, and whose biography is being written by Father Conlan's friend "the Poet"'. Teasing references to a real and imagined past continue to pop up like clues from a game of consequences. Her father was a doctor, and somehow her real brother Edmund (Flora's name for Edwin) had lived in the cottage when he was a boy. When Fiona makes another appearance, she is depicted as a kind of Person from Porlock, interrupting the columnist's Muse. She deposits a wreath of white violets on Flora's terracotta bust of Dante and replaces the typewriter on the writing table with a sewing machine.

Flora's underlining of her fictional counterpart's sensibilities highlights her own longing and nagging sense of unfulfilment. She creates as her alter ego a single, childless woman from a middle-class background living in an idyllic cottage. She could equally well have chosen the person she had been, rather than one she might have been. A literate working-class child from Lark Rise country raising three children in a terraced townhouse would have been as striking a narrator as a doctor's daughter with her head buried in medieval romance. But Flora needed another decade of literary experience before she realized this.

And later still in her life she seemed to become uncomfortable with her invention. In the late 1940s, when she was thinking of gathering her *Catholic Fireside* pieces together in a book, she annotated a section of her June 1921 column with the words 'please leave out'. The offending paragraph contained more details about her fantasy cottage: 'The front of the house is old – very old, as the oak crossbeams and the heavy stone window frames testify, but the long, low-ceilinged parlour at the back was built on some time during the early part of the last century. This room is my real home. Here I have gathered together my books and pictures; the old writing table at which my father wrote out his prescriptions; my grandmother's blue and white china, and the samplers of my great aunts.'

Fiona was not marked for excision. Nor were the increasingly interesting moments when Flora's effusive style (the phrase 'purple patches' has a rather literal meaning where her writing is concerned) begins to approach a kind of magic realism, and edge towards what would eventually become her authentic voice. She eulogizes her old familiars, the telegraph wires, for 'their clear, sharp tautness against the sky', for the way they shine gold in the sun, and confesses that she likes to think of them as a kind of 'golden highway for . . . messages to traverse from friend to absent friend'. In July, when 'the sea had been calling for days', she glimpses 'a trail of wet sword-shaped seaweed glistering across the handlebar of a passing cycle. It was enough.' She muzzles her dog and takes off coastwards.

In August, after inventing a commission from a London botanist to collect 'those tiny, unconsidered florets which grow deep down in the heath turf', she ventures deep into the turf herself and finds it a wonderland that echoed the cosseted retreats of her childhood: 'I crept right under the bracken; the fronds closed around me, and I was in a fairy world. Through the fronds overhead the light filtered greenly; the turf was green velvet; the long stems jade pillars; the tiny golden florets fairy chalices.

There were fungi, too, blood-red, bloated, splashed with yellow, and fairy rings with pearly, half-closed umbrellas.'

*

Despite the ebullience of her columns, and the enchantment offered by 'fairy' (now her favourite adjective) retreats, Flora wasn't happy in 1921. She wrote to a friend in July that 'I have been feeling very low and depressed and have got behind with my work.' There was consolation, of a kind, from her mentor, Ronald Macfie. That year he encouraged Flora to collect together her poems and submit them to the London publishers Philip Allan and Company. *Bog-Myrtle and Peat* came out in the spring at the price of three shillings and sixpence. Flora's choice of title says something about her mood. It's a catchy phrase, but has a melancholy, autumnal edge. Given her frequently expressed feelings, one might have expected her botanical talisman to be the heather that gave her such 'a buoyant, floating-upon-air feeling', the purple robe of Hampshire's 'dark Madonna'. Instead she picked bog myrtle, 'sweet gale', a shrub with an evocative, astringent scent; and peat, the black, decayed remains of living plants which underlay the damp redoubts of the heath.

Bog-Myrtle and Peat can be read as an elegy for Flora's brother Edwin. Its twenty-four verses are unexceptional and derivative, but a sense of loss and absence permeates them. One, 'August Again', refers explicitly to Edwin's violent end in Belgium:

> Ah, very deep my Love must sleep,
> On that far Flemish plain,
> If he does not know that the heath-bells blow
> On the Hampshire hills again!

In 'Home Thoughts from the Desert' she again projects the Hampshire heathlands as a subject of longing. Edwin did know them briefly, when he was stationed in Aldershot, just before leaving for the deserts of the South Africa.

> Amidst the desert sand and heat,
> I hear the wheeling seabirds scream,
> Scent the good smoke of burning peat,
> Then wake and find it but a dream –
> Ah, Hampshire dear!

In 'The Earthly Paradise', a fantasy of rural retreat, she achieves a solidly Georgian quatrain (but, in its declamatory style, also oddly reminiscent of Walt Whitman) and offers a confession about her real desires into the bargain:

> Upon a day of days I would welcome an old poet;
> And pour him tea, and walk upon the heath, and talk
>   the sun down;
> And then by the wood fire he should read me the poems
>   of his passionate youth,
> And make new ones praising friendship above love!

The book attracted a scattering of reviews. Most had faint praise for Flora's poems, but thought she had a talent which was worth encouraging. The *Times Literary Supplement* noted that 'A passion for the open English country – a keen receptiveness to its sights and sounds and scents are the notes of the pieces . . . and they are given adequate and tasteful expression.' The *Evening Standard* praised Thompson's 'charming lyrical faculty' but thought she had more work to do: 'When Miss [*sic*] Thompson disciplines her rather too facile Muse and rejects the easy adjective and the time-worn poetic attitude, she will probably advance considerably on the present volume.'

The *Daily Mirror* printed two photographs of her on its back page for 3 March 1921, the day after the publication. They make a striking pair, and catch the two faces of Flora. One picture has her relaxing back in a chair in front of her considerable typewriter, looking directly at the camera and dressed in a smart two-piece dress with frilly cuffs. (The top appears identical to the one she was wearing for her Grayshott portrait, twenty years before.) A bob haircut and lightweight spectacles add to the impression of an interestingly intellectual and subtly attractive woman. In the other she looks forbiddingly frumpish, encased in an unflattering housecoat and concentrating intently on a mixing basin.

The contrast between earnest hausfrau and sensitive writer was also picked up in a profile in the *Daily Chronicle*, a left-liberal newspaper that was one of the ancestors of the *News Chronicle*. Under a punning headline 'WOMAN OF LETTERS. VILLAGE POSTMISTRESS POETESS', 'Our Own Correspondent, Liphook' quizzes Flora about her writing habits and ambitions. The 'busy mother' bemoaned the difficulty of balancing her literary and domestic roles. 'I started writing little things long ago,' she told the reporter. 'No one helped me, and I have carried on my passion for literature quite alone. In fact, I think I must be the most isolated of women who write poetry . . . I work at my writing when my other housework is done, and how I have found time to do it is a long story. At present I have got a novel in hand. Of course, the central subject is a girl, and it is rather autobiographical. It is almost impossible for one to get away from oneself.' This latter remark the *Chronicle*'s reporter judged to be 'artless'.

Flora's problem at this stage was indeed a kind of artlessness

– not in being too autobiographical in her subjects, but in drawing awkward and impersonal veils across them. Macfie had urged her in the wrong direction. Poetry would never be her *métier*, and *Bog-Myrtle and Peat* was a stylistic cul-de-sac as well as a commercial failure. But Thompson was not ready to let her vitalist idol out of her life. The 'novel in hand', provisionally entitled *Gates of Eden*, concerned a woman called Berengaria,* who is a stonemason's daughter, falling in love with a poet who is also a doctor (though unlike Macfie he is also married, which is Flora's device for keeping her fantasies in check). Flora worked intermittently on this book for much of the 1920s, but she lacked the skills of empathy and character development and plot construction necessary for a sustained work of fiction, and it is a mundane piece, never remotely suitable for publication.

A couple of years later, when she was forty-six, Flora approached *The Catholic Fireside* with another idea, to run alongside her nature column. She proposed that the magazine begin a 'Fireside Reading Circle', a regular feature like the *Lady's Companion* 'Book Club'. Flora would compose a critical essay on a well-known writer or literary school; readers would be invited to enter a competition, in which they would submit their own critical appreciations, or to write more informally to Flora. It was, in many ways, a postal precursor of the modern book club. Flora spelt out its aims in her first essay: 'Let us,

---

* Berengaria was the name of Richard I's wife. But in the 1920s it was better known as the name of an ocean liner, renamed *Berengaria* in 1921, when it was bought by Cunard. If Thompson intended her coining to be a respectful nod towards Macfie's ode on the sinking of the *Titanic*, it had an eerily coincidental postscript. The *Berengaria* caught fire in New York Harbour in 1938 and had to be scrapped.

then, consider ourselves a circle of invisible friends reading the same book at the same time, and each in turn expressing our opinion upon it. In this way we will take the novelists, Dickens and Scott and George Eliot and the Brontës, with many others down to our own day. Some months we will turn aside and study the poets, try to think their thoughts and breathe their atmosphere, until the petty slights and stings of daily life are forgotten, and we gain fresh strength and are inspired to greater effort by their wisdom.'

The first essay, on Sir Walter Scott, appeared in January 1923. Flora prefaces it with some stern remarks on the indiscriminate reading habits of the masses, and – rather richly, given the nature of her own romantic fiction – lambasts 'the lurid atmosphere, the strained pathos, the extravagant luxury ... the exaggerated virtue and vice, which have delighted so many millions of readers and cinema-goers'.

What follows is a competent and conventional survey of Scott's work, much in the style of her diligent student's essay on Jane Austen twelve years before. She sticks to the critical consensus and offers no personal perspectives. Over the next three years she wrote thirty-five such essays – on Dickens, Keats, Robert Louis Stevenson, Thackeray, Meredith and Joseph Conrad and on generic topics such as 'The Poetry of Nature', 'The English Essayists', 'Seaside Reading' and 'Catholic Poets of the Nineteenth Century' (in three parts). She admires robustness in writing, but, reflecting the ethics of her employers and her own uncomfortableness with intense emotions, she is censorious of and sometimes prissy about any deviations from conventional morals.

She describes George Eliot's relationship with G. H. Lewes as 'the one false step in her life we will not concern ourselves with'. She also passes quickly over Shelley's elopement with sixteen-year-old Mary Godwin – 'it is sufficient to say here that he suffered the extreme penalty for his mistaken action'. By the time she had finished the thirty-five essays in November 1925 (the last two were on Rudyard Kipling), Flora may have had an inkling that she was not cut out to be a writer of their kinds of cloth.

Meanwhile, Flora had changed the title of her monthly 'nature' column to the 'Peverel Papers'. The name is something of a mystery. There were Peverills living in Juniper Hill, and two of them are listed alongside Edwin Timms on the war memorial in Cottisford church. *Peveril of the Peak* was a novel by Flora's favourite, Sir Walter Scott. Whatever prompted her, Flora uses the term as a place-name in the construction of yet another literary persona – still fictional, but in terms of location at least, rather closer to her own.

In the first 'Peverel Paper', in January 1922, she announces that she has moved on from the New Forest (though in reality she was still living in Liphook): 'By what we humans call accident, I came upon this cottage, a mere snail-shell of a place, so small and low and grey, tucked away amongst pine and holly at the foot of the Peverel Downs.' This is her invented name for Weavers Down, the heathy slope one mile west of Liphook that was already one of her favourite haunts. But she imagines her discovery of the place – the 'little cell' in its 'peaceful hollow' with 'the blue hills behind, the billowing heath before' – as an unexpected intervention by fate, a moment of benediction. 'I felt like a homing bird after a stormy flight, and could only lie in the grass and fern resting war-worn nerves and steeping my tired soul in the beauty and peace of it all . . . I settled here, a modern hermit, with my dog and my books for company, my garden to supply my frugal table, and my pen to provide my simple luxuries.'

After this mirage of a Hampshire Avalon, which percolates the first few of her 1922 columns, Flora slowly permits her literary *Döppelganger* to dissipate into the haze. Weavers Down, and the other tangible landscapes she was exploring, were too demanding, too *present*, to be traduced by vagueness or fantastical displacements. Her territory now took in the high heaths west and south of Liphook, the bogs and pine forest of Woolmer to the north, and the hanging beech and yew woods between Steep and Selborne, six miles to the west – all of them stitched together by a lacework of prehistoric hollow-ways and chalk slopes and incongruous pools.

8. *The South Country: Flora and the sage of Selborne*

When the poet Hilaire Belloc coined the evocative phrase 'the South Country' for the chalk hill-land between Sussex and Dorset, he was describing a mental journey that was almost the opposite of Flora Thompson's:

> When I am living in the Midlands
>   That are sodden and unkind,
> I light my lamp in the evening:
>   My work is left behind;
> And the great hills of the South Country
>   Come back into my mind.
>
> *from* 'The South Country'

In *Heatherley* Flora describes the air of her Midlands' home country as 'moist, heavy, pollen-laden'. Now she had the wind in the beech trees and the scent of heather. And the particular patch of the south that she was haunting now, strung roughly between Liphook and Alton, had special qualities of compression and convolution. To walk it is to step on a sensory rollercoaster, where glimpsed skylines, sudden dips, hints of water, gaps in woods, succeed each other with disorientating speed. Close to it can be a micro-world of intimate detail and texture: layered sandstone, tree roots contorted around the layers, fungus on the dying trunks above, saplings in the gaps left by fallen trunks. A deep hollow-way, so dense with hazel and ferns that they shut out the light, tops out abruptly to a mile-wide view over chalky fields. You are passing through a gallery of different ways of dwelling, the intense busyness of a meadow tussock suddenly set against the huge slow rhythms of an entire hill.

It would be insulting to suggest that the physical character of a landscape determines the structure and rhythms, as well as the content, of a writer's prose. But it is, inevitably and properly, a strong influence. And it is modulated by being not just direct, but part of a conversation: you're aware that others have walked and watched before you and left their footnotes in the turf – and these fugitive traces of previous witnesses refine the way you see and feel.

Flora knew at least some of the literary provenance of her *terroir*. William Cobbett, out on his *Rural Rides*, had stood on top of one of the plunging, wooded hills in 1822. It was 'like looking from the top of a castle down into the sea'. He had slithered down the muddy sides of the hanger, and taken to one of the deepest hollow lanes, whose towering sandstone walls terrified his horse. 'Talk of *shows*, indeed!' he marvelled, just before getting lost in the dark of Woolmer Forest. 'Take a piece of this road; just a cut across, and a rod long, and carry it up to London. That would be something like a *show*!'

W. H. Hudson had rambled here in the early years of the century, and visited Selborne to listen to the nightingales. Edward Thomas lived near Steep between 1906 and his departure for the Front in 1916. Flora never mentions Thomas's name, but his poetry and his prose work *The South Country* map out the region's intimate weave of prospect and refuge. Flora never comes close to Thomas's startling poetic insights – his thought, for instance, that when 'the lark is high he seems to be singing in some keyless chamber of the brain'. But she would have sympathized with his characterization of their shared country. '[T]he South is tender and will harbour any one; her quiet people resent intrusion quietly, so that many do not notice the resentment. These are the "home" counties. A man can hide away in them. The people are not hospitable, but the land is.'

But Gilbert White was the local writer whom Flora most consciously followed. She passed close to his home village of Selborne on a bus outing one day, but crossed paths with him most weeks. Woolmer Forest, especially its great ponds, was on his regular circuit, as was Weavers Down. Moreover, Flora knew White's *The Natural History of Selborne* (1789) well, having read it at least by the time she was twenty-one, and must have found its rhythms resonating with her as she rambled about the edges of its territory. *Selborne* was a revolutionary work of non-fiction in its day, both in its philosophical stance and its literary adventurousness. There had been books about single villages before, but none which included all species in their roll-call of parishioners, and which accorded house-crickets the same detailed and respectful attention as home-owners.

White had used contemporary fictional devices, too. The book is in the 'epistolary style', and framed as a set of conversational letters to two colleagues. They are datelined 'Selborne', adding to their sense of rootedness in a specific time and place. Some of the letters are imaginary, in the sense that they are essays done up as correspondence but never actually sent. Many are quarried from a 'Naturalist's Journal' that White kept almost continuously for more than thirty-five years. In this he developed a spare haiku-like style, in which his attention repeatedly changes focus, from immediate foreground to supporting backdrop. This is an entry for 4 June

1785: 'Several halo's & mock suns this morning. Wheat looks black, & gross. Crickets sing much on the hearth this evening: they feel the influence of moist air, & sing against rain. As the great wall-nut tree has no foliage this year, we have hung the meat-safe on Miss White's Sycomore, which she planted a nut.' The discursive route White's narrative shuttle follows here is astonishing, managing to weave together several decades of tree growth, extraordinary weather, harvest prospects, human culinary customs and hearth-crickets' music in just over fifty words. His ability to show the links that held communities together, across species and back over time, is part of White's intrinsic genius. But it was facilitated in no small measure by the convoluted landscape of the Hampshire Weald.

In one of his rambling letters to Thomas Pennant in *Selborne*, White is chatting amicably about the eating habits of young owls and the house-martins he had glimpsed in Oxford early in the winter. Then he breaks off, almost apologetically, and attempts to explain this stream of discursive ornithology. 'The parish I live in', he writes, 'is a very abrupt uneven country, full of hills and woods, and therefore full of birds.'

*

It's in the more acutely observed of her Hampshire journals that Flora, at last, begins to give clues as to the kind of author she is destined to become. One particular day in November 1921 she is meandering in the local woods, gathering copy for her column. She walked most mornings, after seeing the children off to school, beginning to snuffle through the undergrowth of her own childhood memories as avidly as through the autumn leaf-litter: a cub author in every sense.

That morning, her dog Boojie (its 'bohemian' nom de plume: its real name was Prince) had its nose speared by a hedgehog, and she had toyed with epithets for the autumn colour show. She liked early winter, the sense of a small rite of seasonal passage – '"The Little Festival of the Toasting Fork", as we, as children, used to call the first tea . . . by lamplight'. Then the day took a lucky, romantic turn. She met a gypsy gathering wood-sage, a stately, undeferential woman of eighty-nine. 'She was gorgeously and uniquely clad,' Flora wrote, 'in a man's crimson quilted dressing gown, finished with hobnailed, steel-tipped boots.' She told Flora's fortune, without even the perk of a palm crossed with silver: '"It's the face," she said, "not the hand. It's all writ in the face what a person is. And, if I know what you are, I can tell pretty well how things'll go with you!" She was certainly able to read the secret desire, for she promised me love and praise and friendship! "You are goin' to be loved," she said, "loved by a lot o' folks – strangers shall become friends – people all over –" and she waved her bundle of wood-sage to include the entire horizon. Nonsense, of course! Yet after I parted from her, I trod more lightly, and strange to say, when I reached home I found a letter awaiting me from a complete stranger praising some trifle I had written.'

This passage is self-revealing and doesn't disguise Flora's aching ambition. There is a hint of self-mocking, and of credulity. There are themes, too, that she will return to again: the fascination with clothing, the glamorous life of the gypsy, who lived with one hobnailed foot in wild nature and the other in a world of fable and mystery.

The 'Hermit of Peverel' remains in florid and fantasizing mode through the late winter of 1922, inviting a gypsy girl into her non-existent cottage, wallowing in her acquisition of sixteen volumes of Browning, and doing Mass Observation on Christmas shoppers: 'If I were a millionaire I should spend whole days taking slum children into toyshops, workmen's wives into milliners' and poor poets into bookshops. I should recognize the latter at a glance, because in their eyes the longing is raised to the *n*th degree.'

Then in May, something happens, and a more exacting, attentive note enters Flora's otherwise scatty narratives. She is watching two cuckoos, and notices one maverick individual, 'a bachelor-like kind of creature, which makes its headquarters in the dead upper branches of a lightning-stricken oak upon the edge of the heath'. She is listening 'minutely' too, and realizes he has an idiosyncratic call – 'Cuck-cuck-cuck-oo'. She becomes increasingly alert to *particularity*, and that this means something about the richness of an organism's (a human's included) experience. The poet in her watches blue butterflies dropping down and 'threading themselves' in silhouette on a grass stalk, 'until they look like some new and strange flower'; and the naturalist wonders how the dust of their wings survives rainfall.

Her writing is now becoming extravagantly discursive and she begins to look at everything – foxes, oak trees, shepherds, cakes in shops – with the same rapt fascination. Soon she can look at a swallow with an intensity that makes it seem quite new-minted. Its colour 'was neither black nor blue, but an indescribably rich shade of violet, with underparts of a pearly pink, glowing to pale flame about the breast. More striking still than the actual tints was the bright burnish, which made the whole of its plumage look newly-varnished.'

Increasingly she is (like White) not just absorbing the look of things, but asking how they function, how they fit with each other. She works her way through the bloody spectacle of a kestrel-kill to an understanding of its necessity for the falcon, and a comparison with our own slaughter of animals for food. She empathizes with the brief life-experience of mayfly, seeming an ephemeral and meaningless waste to us, but from the insect's perspective, a whole existence devoted to a 'dance in the sun'. Flora isn't just a distant watcher. She is standing up for her point of view too, at least in print. She rails against otter-hunting and the destruction of hedgerows. A gamekeeper turfs her out of an 'earthly paradise', an enchanted bower 'of white and blue and gold' by a brook, and she argues (later, in her column: she goes meekly from the wood) for the right to wander 'where one would' in the countryside. 'For one man to lay claim to a primrose wood or a bluebell dell and to pay another man to watch it is an outrage upon the rest of humanity.'

These enclosed, 'fairy' enclaves figure strongly in the 'Peverel Papers'. But they've progressed from being echoes of the hide-aways Flora dreamed of as a child. They've become focal points in the landscape, where her dawning understanding of the idea of 'natural community' is being distilled and condensed. She walks on the heath 'in a small enclosed world a dozen paces in diameter' and notices the different colours in the vegetation which have been made by successions of rain and frost. An ancient beech, 'the Grey Lady', now fallen, had created 'a perfect bower, a green mansion of shade' under which humans too formed brief associations. Children called it 'the house' and made furniture of moss and twigs to arrange amongst the roots. Adults sheltered from showers under the foliage. Now the trunk and branches have been cleared away, new vegetation will spring up in the uninterrupted sunlight. '"Change, change, for ever change,"' Flora quotes, '"change and decay"'. Even the heath's ancient trackways become arenas for this historical process. 'Sometimes I follow these deserted paths, winding in and out to skirt the hills and the marshes, just as they were first trodden by the naked feet of primitive man.'

The journals are not always this weighty. Fiona makes a couple more brief appearances, and extracts a promise from Flora that she will give up for ever her 'suicidal menu' of foraged fungi. But Fiona is now presented as such a ridiculous figure you feel Flora is poking a little farewell fun at the whole exotic persona – the emotionally wounded doctor's daughter – that she invented for herself at the start of the 'Peverel Papers'.

For Gilbert White, though, she has unqualified affection, and perhaps a touch of envy. In February 1923 she wonders if, a century and a half apart, they had watched the same rookery on Weavers Down. 'It is easy to imagine him, the very first of English nature writers, with his powdered hair and sober clerical garb, jogging along the road on his fat grey mare, stopping beneath the elms to gaze upwards at the noisy black birds about their business of nest-making, lingering perhaps to jot down a date or caress some early spray of blackthorn with his riding whip; then jogging homeward away over Peverel, the most sober and modest, yet happiest, of men!'

Flora was now absorbing more serious natural history through her reading, and the deepening understanding behind her observations begins to give them the kind of metaphorical power Gilbert White's work often possesses. Sometimes, as he did, she pushes the analogies close to the edge of anthropomorphism, as in an account of the habits of black ants. 'One very touching incident in ant-life takes place when the female, back from her marriage flight, prepares to make a home for the coming generation. The first thing she does is to nip off her own wings lest she should be tempted to disport herself in the sunshine, to the detriment of her maternal duties. There is something very human about this action, as many of my readers who are mothers will understand. I wondered no modern novelist has taken it for a text' (cf. her remarks on dodder, p. 74). But she isn't strictly suggesting that ant mothers are like human mothers. Rather, she is using her own experience as a mother to intuit something about the universal experience of raising a new generation.

In Flora's best sketches, the metaphors are more implicit, and their strength comes from this attentiveness to (and now knowledge of) the processes and challenges common to all life. This is her fine reflection on mosses, from January 1927: 'Long before the higher forms of vegetation could find foothold on the naked rock of the newly-cooled earth's surface the mosses came and throve through countless generations, each small tuft drawing its sustenance from the air, attracting and holding together the dusty particles washed down by the rains, dying and leaving behind it the residue of its decay, until soil enough had collected for higher vegetable life to flourish in. *Servi*, or labourers, the great botanist Linnaeus called the mosses – a name of honour.' It's no surprise that memories of the hard-working community she had grown up with in Oxfordshire soon begin to be re-imagined in the Hampshire heathlands. In one of the final 'Peverel Papers', a character sketch of the Lark Rise 'bee-wife', Queenie Macey (see pp. 17–18), makes its first appearance.

*

Flora had always wanted to live in the real countryside, rather than in a Post Office annexe, and early in 1926 she noticed that there was a newly built house for sale in the hamlet of Griggs Green, on the Longmoor Road between Liphook and Greatham, and, more importantly, just a few minutes' walk from the foot of Weavers Down. John no longer had night-time duties at the Liphook switchboard and readily agreed to Flora's plan to move there. He raised a mortgage of £675, and they took possession in July.

The house is still there, a smart, three-bedroomed villa with a red-tiled roof, set amidst pine trees. Flora, as was her custom, immediately dubbed it 'Woolmer Gate', after the one-time deer-forest of Woolmer, of which Weavers Down was a part, and whose other remnants (already beginning to be invaded by Forest Service conifers) lay to the north of the house. Flora discovered that the house carried with it commoner's rights over the forest, so she was able to gather dead and fallen wood for the fire, provided she didn't use an 'axe or billhook to lop stick or stock'.

Flora was in her element at last, and began to relish the role of 'Twenties Countrywoman'. Her next-door neighbour Joe Leggett recalls that her sense of appropriate fashion hadn't deserted her: 'she would appear in a very smart blue Burberry raincoat, a waterproof hat of the same material and button-up footwear that reached well above the ankles. In better weather she usually wore a skirt and blouse; nothing gaudy, but always in good taste.' She took her dog, Prince, packed a Thermos flask (a comparatively new accessory), and strode off for Weavers Down. We know the route she took because, since becoming a minor local celebrity with the publication of *Bog-Myrtle and Peat*, she had been invited to write a guidebook to the area: 'To reach Weavers Down, leave the Longmoor Road at The Deer's Hut [a public house], and take the footpath which passes its doorway. Just a fringe is left there of the old primeval forest oak and holly and immemorial yew, but very soon this is left behind and the open heath of which Woolmer at this day chiefly consists lies spread before the wayfarer . . .

the geologist, naturalist or beauty-lover will each find a happy hunting ground there, and one that has scarcely been touched since Gilbert White wrote of it.'

Flora continued to write 'Peverel Papers' for *The Catholic Fireside* and tutor her readers. But she wanted to do more for those who were hopeful of becoming writers themselves. So she brought the 'Fireside Reading Circle' to an end in 1925 and began planning her own postal writers' group, to explore the educational potential of the business she had once worked in. She had become friendly with one of the regular contributors to the Circle's competitions, the splendidly named Mildred Humble-Smith. Mildred (or Myldrede, as she called herself in print) had enjoyed the benefits of a formal higher education. She had studied English at Oxford at a time when the university still refused to grant degrees to women, and instead had picked up degrees from both Edinburgh and Durham universities.

Together the two women launched 'The Peverel Society' in November 1925, with an advertisement in *The Catholic Fireside*. Ronald Macfie persuaded Lady Margaret Sackville to become patron (her burst of spite towards Flora (see p. 99) was many years in the future), and the aims of the society were outlined in a brochure sent to all members. For an annual subscription of 7s 6d, they could receive courses, written chiefly by Flora, on verse-writing, short stories, and literary techniques in general. They responded by submitting one piece of writing each month. The secretary (Humble-Smith) divided the entries into groups, based on the members' individual needs, and made up a portfolio, which was circulated to all the members of the group, until all who wished to had read and commented on each entry. Flora made the final evaluation.

At one point up to a dozen portfolios were circulating

around the country, and members began communicating directly with one another. The Society encouraged this. One of its advertisements began 'There is no need to be lonely. The Peverel Society offers sympathetic criticism to literary aspirants. New friendships and new interest to all'. One development was the prophetically named 'Chats Book', which answered marketing queries and provided a site for discussion between members.

But Flora was determined to keep the focus on literature, and if the Peverel Society could be portrayed as an early experiment in social networking, it was more obviously an outgrowth of the educationally and scientifically respectable 'exchange' societies which had begun to flourish in the Victorian era. These encouraged members to use the postal system to circulate specimens (plants, rocks, insects all did the rounds) for examination and discussion. For Flora (who, incidentally, had now joined the Haslemere Microscope and Natural History Society), the Peverel Society was one of the good things made possible by her one-time occupation and what she approvingly describes as 'modern machinery', and was an example of how her life, like her books, was an attempt to put a bridge between the best bits of tradition and innovation.

★

Flora's sojourn at the foot of Weavers Down was brief. In 1927, John Thompson saw an advertisement for a postmaster's job in Dartmouth, Devon. He had grown up by the sea on the Isle of Wight, and having acceded to Flora's desire to live in her beloved Hampshire for the past decade, perhaps he felt it was his turn for a spell on familiar turf. But when he was appointed in August 1927, at a salary of £215 per annum, Flora was appalled, shocked that her husband could think of uprooting the family so soon after they had moved to Griggs Green. She dug in her heels and declined to accompany him until Woolmer Gate was sold and he had found a permanent replacement.

The following twelve months were some of Flora's happiest. She was always comfortable in her own company, and may have been relieved to be away from John for a while after his hurtful, and unilateral, decision. Her two oldest children were grown up, though still living with her, and the youngest, Peter, was already nine. For the first time since she was married Flora was comparatively free to do what she liked. She laboured to give Woolmer Gate a real cottage garden, though she knew it would be others who enjoyed it. She worked desultorily on the draft of *Gates of Eden*. And, for a while at least, she continued to write her 'Peverel Papers'. The last column appeared in December 1927, and her long relationship with *The Catholic Fireside* ended.

In July 1928, Woolmer Gate was finally sold, and a couple of months later John returned briefly to collect his family and take them down to the house he had found in Dartmouth. A piqued Flora wrote a mournful note about their departure from Hampshire one rain-drenched autumn day: 'My last glimpse of the snug little red-tiled cottage with a backing of pine trees which had been our home was one of desolation. Trees dripped heavily, the lawn before the house was a swamp and the flowers left in the border were dropping and draggled . . . even my momentary pause beside the grave of an old dog [Prince, aka Boojie] produced a chorus of expostulation from the assembled and waiting family.'

9. The Making of Laura

The house that awaited them was called 'The Outlook'. It was a crow's nest of a place in an area of Dartmouth called Above Town, and had dramatic views over the River Dart, which flowed out through wooded hills towards the Channel. Flora quickly found that the spot had compensations. Behind the house were woods full of primroses and wood anemones and bluebells. Below it, she could walk to where the Dart flowed into the sea and lose herself in a landscape of rock pools and shingle banks of a kind she'd had little experience of before. John seemed inclined to cosset her, after dragging her unwillingly out of her knowledge. He built her a special room for writing in their steeply sloping garden. And despite now owning his own retreat (a boat called the *Sea Mew*) he made time to visit Dartmoor with her (30 miles away by road). The moor wasn't Hampshire, but it had heather and wide open spaces. And it had the dwarf and 'faery' oaks of Wistman's Wood, which enchanted Flora.

Flora's writing marked time during these early Devon years. She continued her work for the Peverel Society. She toyed with a little poetry, including a solemn valedictory ode to Macfie, who died suddenly in a London nursing home in 1931. None of it was published. More bizarrely she responded to an advertisement in a literary journal for a ghost-writer for a retired big-game hunter. Perhaps her desperate need for money was tinged with affectionate memories of her 'Heatherley' friend, the elephant-potting 'Mr Foreshaw'. At any rate, during the early

1930s she put together stories of bloody colonial adventuring for the *Scottish Field*, *Chambers's Journal* and various African newspapers. It may have been a journeyman job that troubled her conscience. A decade earlier she had written passionate denouncements of hunting and shooting and even butterfly-collecting in her 'Peverel' columns. She had been appalled by the landlord of a village inn, who had a stuffed kingfisher in a case above the bar. 'I do not think I should care to meet', Flora wrote, 'the man who could find it in his heart to slay so much beauty and to keep the stuffed body in an atmosphere of stale beer and bad tobacco.'

One day early in 1935, Flora sat in her writing room jotting notes in a diary. In the space for Monday, 21 January, she scribbled 'Waly, waly, wallflower growing up so high, we are all maidens so we must die' – a stanza from a children's playground chant she remembered from Juniper Hill. It is one of her few journal notes to survive and suggests she was pondering where, as a writer, she went next. She had on her mind the positive reaction she'd had from *Catholic Fireside* readers whenever she wrote of rural life in Victorian Oxfordshire. 'The feature most liked in the articles', she recalled, almost casually, 'were my sketches of old country life and characters, remembered from my childhood, and I determined that in some future time I would describe them more fully.' After five years in which she had published almost nothing, that time seemed to have arrived.

The national mood was certainly favourable to the kind of sketches – documentaries with just a touch of yearning romanticism – that Flora was beginning to write. The uneasy truce in Europe, the prolonged economic depression, the sense of an insidious cultural suburbanism, nurtured a widespread yearning for all things rural during the 1920s and 30s. It was not strictly nostalgic, because there was a real sense that the old ruralism could be reshaped for modern needs. Stanley Baldwin (later leader of the Conservative majority in the National Government in the 1930s) set the tone in a 1924 speech, 'What England means to me', that could have been an early 'Peverel Paper'. 'The wild anemones in the woods in April, the last load at night of hay being drawn down a lane as the twilight comes on, when you can scarcely distinguish the figures of the horses as they take it home to the farm, and above all, most subtle, most penetrating and most moving, the smell of wood smoke coming up in an autumn evening, or the smell of the scutch fires: that wood smoke that our ancestors, tens of thousands of years ago, must have caught on the air when they were coming home with the result of the day's forage . . .'

The countryside seemed a place where the fractured historical roots of a troubled nation might still be intact, or at least most readily mended; and where the flavoursome accents and idiosyncrasies of life might have survived the remorseless advance of uniformity. In 1927 H. V. Morton published a bestselling travel book and called it *In Search of England*. But it was really a search for many Englands – for the local, the particular, for the remarkable diversity of life and landscape that was crammed into a small island. A diffuse rural longing touched all arts and media, high and low. Country rambling became a craze, helped by the expansion of the railway system. E. M. Forster wrote and produced a pageant called 'England's Pleasant Land', celebrating the thousand-year history of his Surrey village. John Piper went on 'church crawls' and documented medieval village architecture in watercolour. The folk-song revival became more democratic, embracing twentieth-century and even urban material. The young BBC was supportive, and ran in-the-field recordings of named singers.

Gilbert White, too, was rediscovered as an authentic voice from village England, speaking not in the tones of some stock yokel, but lyrically, intelligently, inclusively, about the particularities of place. The country writer and polemicist H. J. Massingham collaborated with the artist Eric Ravilious on an illustrated collection of White's writings in 1938. He thought *Selborne* was 'the supreme voice of the English parish', and an example to those 'who have lost the art of distinguishing one place from another'. Virginia Woolf admired not just White's content, but his literary technique (which Thompson was learning to echo) – the framing of the intimate close-up against the wider landscape, the counterpoint between the particular and the universal. Woolf noted that White's 'observation of the insect in the grass is minute' but he then raises his eyes to the horizon in a 'moment of abstraction'. This was writing reflecting ecology.

In the USA, also gripped by depression, there was a rural revival too. And one key character in it had a life that almost eerily reflected Flora's. During the 1920s, an Ozark Mountains farmer's wife called Laura Ingalls Wilder wrote a column on country matters, housekeeping and, just occasionally, politics for *The Missouri Ruralist*. In 1932, when she was sixty-five, she published the first title in the classic *Little House on the Prairie* series. This, as *Lark Rise* would eventually be, was a memoir of childhood, in which recollections of 'old country ways' (in this case of a life in a covered wagon in the wilds of the Midwest) are braided with fond memories of the clarity of a young person's imaginative vision. It has as its main character a young girl called Laura, who helps recount the story in the third person. And this Laura, too, hears larks on the prairie . . .

Flora was part of this movement by the logic of who she was, as much as from any deliberate social commitment. In 1936 she wrote a few slight stories and articles with a seaside setting under the pen-name of Frances Stuart Thompson. Then she dug out a story she had written in Liphook years before, called 'The Tail-less Fox'. It differed from her earlier fiction in being set not in some manorial farm or big house but a dirt-poor cottage, and featured a working-class mother who gives birth to her sixth child while her 'hands were still sodden and corrugated from her morning at the washtub'.

Out of what was now a gathering sense of purpose and focus, Flora sent it to *The Lady*. It appeared in December 1936. She followed it next April with an essay on 'Old Queenie', reworking material from 'The Peverel Papers' and from her manuscript for *Gates of Eden*. Three months later she approached *The National Review* with an essay about Juniper Hill, entitled 'An Oxfordshire Hamlet in the Eighties'. During the winter of 1937–8, buoyed up by the prospect of a rare visit from her son Basil (recently married in America) as well as by her new bout of productivity, she wrote another piece for the same magazine on 'May Day in the Eighties', which was published in May 1938.

The idea of a book about her childhood was now firmly on her agenda. During 1938 she began redrafting the recent essays, sensing that at last she had found her voice. Her original 'May Day' essay had begun with a paragraph about court ladies 'going a-maying', a last toying with the streak of feyness that had always bedevilled her writing. Now, against a background of growing national unease about the possibility of war, she sat down and rewrote it. The new opening roots the story in winter, and in an exhilarating, windswept evocation of the rites of passage into spring: 'After the excitement of the concert came the long winter months, when snowstorms left patches on the ploughed fields, like scrapings of sauce on left-over pieces of Christmas pudding, until the rains came and washed them away and the children, carrying old umbrellas to school, had them turned inside out by the wind, and cottage chimneys smoked and washing had to be dried indoors. But at last came spring and spring brought May Day, the greatest day in the year from the children's point of view.'

The insights from Hampshire and Gilbert White, and the hard work of turning them into prose, were paying off. She had come to appreciate intellectually the complex links that held all living communities together, and that to portray these needed an exact and respectful attention to detail. Her essays for *The Lady* and *The National Review* showed just this. In 'May Day' she details how a dim echo of rural Catholicism survived in backroom inventiveness and inter-village rivalries: '[T]he children assembled at six o'clock on May Day morning. Then a large china doll in a blue frock was brought forth from the depths of the school needlework chest and arranged in a sitting position on a little ledge in the centre front of the garland. This doll was known as "the lady", and a doll of some kind was considered essential. Even in those parishes where the garland had degenerated into a shabby nosegay carried aloft at the top of a stick, some dollish image was mixed in with the flowers. The attitude of the children to the lady is interesting. It was understood that the garland was her garland, carried in her honour. The lady must never be roughly handled. If the garland turned turtle, as it was apt to do later in the day, when the road was rough and the bearers were growing weary, the first question was always, "Is the lady all right?"'

The rather casual opportunism with which Flora had embarked on her Oxfordshire essays early in 1935 had blossomed into what the Welsh call *awen*, fluency of inspiration. She was bursting with creative energy, each new idea nudging the next into place, a long jigsaw puzzle at last being solved. There was, first, the challenge of establishing a point of view. Her magazine articles on Juniper Hill had no narrator, so she invented and inserted 'Laura', to provide a 'child's eye' and a developing character in the story. Laura was partly Flora's younger self, but like the narrator she had created for her 'Out of Doors' column, also a fictional persona, a protective skin. Flora 'dressed up' in these invented characters to disguise her emotional awkwardness, and to live out her imaginings: in the case of the 'Hermit of Peverel', of the mysterious romantic she might have been; in the case of 'Laura', the child she had left behind. But 'Laura' soon developed into someone more substantial than a fantastical alter ego: she was an interpreter, who would translate Flora's memories into the vivid sensual language of her childhood.

Laura was an unprompted inspiration but perfectly in tune with the revisions Flora now made to her first *National Review* essay, 'An Oxfordshire Hamlet in the Eighties'. The version in the magazine had begun with a conventionally objective sentence: 'The hamlet stood on a gentle rise in that flat corn-growing part of the country which was dignified by the name of "the hill".' The newly energized Flora, scenting the opening moment of her book, scotches this and writes instead its famous opening paragraph: 'The hamlet stood on a gentle rise in the flat, wheat-growing north-east corner of Oxfordshire. We will call it Lark Rise because of the great number of skylarks which made the surrounding fields their spring-board and nested on the bare earth between the rows of green corn.'*

And suddenly the story takes wing, becomes buoyant, as Flora herself did when she first truly perceived a landscape from the outside, on the Hampshire hills forty years before. It isn't just the rising larks that lift the reader, but the swooping panoramic view, and the power of that inclusive pronoun, 'we'. *We* are no longer remote outsiders but equal witnesses of the story with Laura.

It's impossible to say where Flora got the idea for this textual flourish, but it is a familiar one, not so much in literature as in film. It is a voice-over, the reflections and reminiscences of a narrator uttered alongside what is actually happening on the screen. (Memorable examples were the opening and closing sequences of *The Waltons*, the 1970s US film and television series set in a poor Virginia farming community during the Depression.) It establishes the possibility of two time-frames (and the two identities, Flora and Laura) running alongside each other: an account of what happened, and a judgement on it, possibly ornamented, made later.

Flora couldn't sustain the levitation, the arms-open-in-welcomeness of that first paragraph. But every author knows that a book's character – and its readers' reactions – can swing

---

* There was a real field called Lark Rise in the real Juniper Hill. But, in the late 1930s, Flora's choice of this airy place and its attendant birds to be both the title of her book and the motif of its defining first paragraph cannot fail to have been influenced by the symbolic importance of the skylark in the 'war to end all wars' twenty-five years before. Vaughan Williams's lyric tone-poem 'The Lark Ascending' was written in 1914. The lark was the totemic bird of the trenches. In its song the poets of the Great War heard England, home and survival. And larks are there, along with the Flanders Field poppies, in the bitter verse of John McCrae that was to inspire Remembrance Day.

on the fulcrum of its opening. It is safe to say that *Lark Rise* would have had a different future if we hadn't been there with Flora from the outset, and complicit with her in claiming and naming the hamlet as a kind of shared motherlode.

Central to the success of *Lark Rise to Candleford* is the figure of Laura. Laura is an avatar, a semi-fictionalized version of Flora's young self. She never narrates the story, but is the chief character in it. She allows Flora to express what in a conventional memoir would be straightforward first-person statements, with more surreptitious, ambivalent asides, almost like counterpoint.

What adds more layers of interest to the story are the different roles played by Laura in the three volumes that make up the book, which are often treated as if they were similar kinds of narrative. The first, *Lark Rise*, is the least complicated, a story whose chief focus is the village community, its pattern of work and social relations. Laura is introduced as a character (as are her family) but her role is analogous to that of a Shakespearean chorus. Flora tells most of the story as a reminiscing adult, but presents Laura's view when she wants to lighten the tone of an episode, or show it through the vivid, unmediated vision of a girl. Sometimes the viewpoints of adult and child are deliberately played against each other, with a kind of wry dramatic irony.

Laura, aged twelve, witnesses a cow and bull *in flagrante*, but it is the post-Freudian Flora who comments 'the sight did not warp her nature. She neither peeped from behind a rick, nor fled, horrified across country; but merely thought in her old-fashioned way, "Dear me! I had better slip quietly away before the men see me."' Flora presents Laura as hyper-sensitive and daringly adventurous by turns. The frequently quoted story of the annual pig-killing is told with a stark realism that is both grown-up and oddly childlike, but Laura and the other village children unquestionably *cope* with it and have a ravenous appetite for the gristly outer covering of the toes, known as 'shoes'. And Laura is the first person in the hamlet to eat tomatoes, that truly foreign food: '. . . the basket of red and yellow fruit attracted Laura's colour-loving eye. "What are those?" she asked old Jerry. "Love-apples, me dear. Love-apples they be; though some hignorant folks be a callin' 'em tommytoes. But you don't want any o' they – nasty sour things, they be, as only gentry can eat . . ." But Laura felt she must taste the love-apples and insisted upon having one.' Flora, tongue in cheek no doubt, having presented her adolescent self as tasting the forbidden fruit, ends with a mundane retrospective note, remarking that those childhood fruits had a flavour far preferable to 'the watery insipidity of our larger, smoother tomato'.

The book ends with Queen Victoria's Golden Jubilee in 1887, and with a new, poignant tone of voice. The celebrations seemed (to Flora looking back, I suspect, not Laura at the time) to mark a moment of change. Reaping machines and the first 'offcomers' arrive in the hamlet. 'People began to speak of "before the Jubilee" much as we in the nineteen-twenties spoke of "before the war", either as a golden time or as one of exploded ideas, according to the age of the speaker.'

Then Flora mentions the Great War itself, still nearly three decades in the future. 'And all the time boys were being born or growing up in the parish, expecting to follow the plough all their lives, or, at most, to do a little mild soldiering or go to work in a town. Gallipoli? Kut? Vimy Ridge? Ypres? What did they know of such places? But they were to know them, and when the time came they did not flinch. Eleven out of that tiny community never came back again. A brass plate on the wall of the church immediately over the old end house seat is engraved with their names. A double column, five names long, then, last and alone, the name of Edmund.'

The name on the brass plaque is in fact that of Edwin, Flora's beloved brother and constant childhood companion. This is as close as she comes to acknowledging the autobiographical basis of *Lark Rise*, but it is also a sophisticated literary move, inserting a foreknowledge of the future into what had previously been a seemingly straightforward record of the past. This device, in which the author hints at what is going to happen to her characters before they know themselves, recurs throughout her books.

In the second volume, *Over to Candleford*, Laura herself becomes the chief character, and the form of the narrative more closely resembles a conventional novel. We learn about her extended family, both in Lark Rise and the surrounding villages and towns. She makes visits to them, her first opportunities to leave her native hamlet. And her horizons expand in other ways, from her mother's storytelling and her own unquenchable passion for reading. In a nod of literary respect to Laura's developing maturity, Flora fleshes out the characters in *Over to Candleford* and they have more substantial and nuanced personalities than the briefly sketched cast of *Lark Rise*.

Laura is growing up, and out, and her role is subtly changing from sharp observer of village life to someone reflecting on the rites of passage to adulthood, a novelist in embryo. In the penultimate chapter of the book, just before she leaves the hamlet for ever, Laura approaches the winter in a mood of sullen, adolescent brooding. But one unpromising November morning, she is suddenly lifted, as she will be repeatedly over the years to come, by the exceptionalness of the commonplace: a flock of starlings whirring from a bush, the mist condensing in bright beads of water at the tips of the ivy-leaves. Nature was already a refuge for Laura in a way that people would never be.

In *Candleford Green* she has finally left home, to take up a position as a postal assistant in the nearby village of that name (as we have seen, it's modelled chiefly on Fringford, a village south-east of Juniper Hill, though Flora freely admits that she has melded her experience of several villages). Laura is now maturing into a young woman under the emancipated wing of postmistress Dorcas Lane, who introduces her to contemporary writers and encourages her to acquire white-collar skills. Candleford Green is a village which, like Laura, is in a state of change, slowly evolving into a kind of suburb, and nurturing a new social class 'on the borderline between the working and middle classes'.

Laura expresses mixed feelings about these people, and the trade-off they have made between old values and a better standard of living. But she has no qualms about moving on to join their company, and in the last paragraphs of the book, Flora has her alter ego go through a symbolic rite of graduation, embracing both what she has learned and what she has still to look forward to. As she walks away from Candleford Green, Laura looks back at its familiar landmarks: 'the little birch thicket where the long-tailed tits had congregated, the boathouse where she had sheltered from the thunderstorm . . . and the hillock beyond from which she had seen the perfect rainbow. She was never to see any of these again, but she was to carry a mental picture of them, to be recalled at will, through the changing scenes of a lifetime. As she went on her way, gossamer threads, spun from bush to bush, barricaded her pathway, and as she broke through one after another of these fairy barricades she thought, "They're trying to bind and keep me". But the threads which were to bind her to her native county were more enduring than gossamer. They were spun of love and kinship and cherished memories.'

Margaret Lane, Flora's first biographer, has pondered the elasticity of those threads of memory and affection. Flora Thompson, she wrote, 'was able to write the annals of the poor because she was one of them'. Perhaps '*had* been one of them' would have been more accurate. By the time she wrote the annals of Lark Rise, Flora Thompson was distantly removed from it by geography, class, self-education and wealth. Perhaps that is what gave her, at last, a perspective on her roots, and a voice in which to commemorate them. What is remarkable, and a piece of literary legerdemain, is that the voice sounds as if it is speaking directly from the time it describes.

Lark Rise to Candleford is often described as – and occasionally rebuked for being – a work in the 'pastoral' tradition, one of the vaguer and more contentious genres in literature. Its simplest definition is 'a form of escape literature concerned with country pleasures'. More hostile views suggest that it is a kind of writing in which the hard realities of rural life and work are obscured by idyllic and Arcadian stereotypes: musical shepherds, contented cottagers, fieldwork and field-play for everyone. Often there is the qualification that pastoral is prose or poetry celebrating the countryside which has been composed by those who are not part of it. Raymond Williams, in *The Country and the City* (written in 1973 but still one of the most intelligent and sympathetic critiques of rural writing), suggests that the weakness of most rural literature of the first half of the twentieth century is that the writers '*came to* the country' from urban England, Bloomsbury, the universities;

the 'nerves were already strained, the minds already formed'. Many were acute and sensitive observers, and saw and understood things passed over by 'the natives'. But too often their insights were smothered under misplaced classical references and intellectual fantasies about 'the Folk' and Old England.

What was special about Flora Thompson is that she *came from* the country. Her direct experience and sharp observations of village and field were already embedded, long before her maturing literary sensibilities got to work on them – which is to return to the counterpoint and contrast between her own life-story and the tale she chose, or felt most driven, to tell. A life as it was lived and a life as it was told. Both dreams of a good life, but not the same life. Perhaps it is the play of one dream on the other that makes *Lark Rise to Candleford* still resonant today.

The interplay is intricate. There are inventions and roundings-off throughout the text of *Lark Rise*. Characters are shifted out of one place or time-frame and insinuated into another – all of which could be seen as attempts by Flora to portray the hamlet community as more idyllic and self-reliant than it was. The critic Barbara English logs a daunting number of *Lark Rise*'s historical solecisms. Flora, for instance, describes the hamlet as a static community. 'Nobody goes away' was a local saying which she repeats with approval. 'This assertion,' English suggests, 'which would certainly make Juniper Hill unique in late nineteenth-century England, can be shown to be untrue.' Villagers came and went, some being present at one decennial census, missing at the next, and returning in the third. Only thirteen of the families in the 1881 census had been in the hamlet in 1871. And Flora herself, of course, 'went away' in 1891, never to return.

Barbara English is most struck by the downplaying of death in Flora's narrative. The only deaths recorded are those of elderly people. High infant and child mortality – one of the defining features of Victorian poverty – is simply not mentioned, let alone discussed, despite the fact that four of Flora's siblings died under the age of three. Was this the hard-headedness of the dirt-poor, a kind of rural fatalism? An acceptance that there was a natural cull of children just as there was of stock (though the annual slaughter of the pig is not ignored and is spelt out in grimly realistic detail)? Perhaps this is Flora being true to Laura's youthful vision of the blameless little ones being taken back to God (though at the time she wrote it she was living in suburban comfort and had already lost a child of her own, so might be expected to be more sensitive to loss).

Barbara English argues, to the contrary, that this and all the other omissions of hard or unglamorous facts are quite deliberate: '*Lark Rise* is not an artless production, rather a very skilful piece of special pleading. Thompson told her story with a purpose: the changes of fact or changes of emphasis . . . were made in order to reinforce her theme. For she too was caught up in the "Old England" legend.' 'Whatever her aims and intention may have been,' English concludes, 'she constructed a past which never really existed. Blurred, softened by the art of the writer, *Lark Rise* resembles those memories of childhood where the sun shone all summer, and there was always snow at Christmas.'

Published in the politically charged mid-1980s, this essay was itself a piece of special pleading, the orthodox contemporary historian's view that life in nineteenth-century rural England was nasty, brutish and often very short, and that to argue otherwise was to excuse a whole raft of exploitation by landowners, from the manipulation of rent and wage levels to the prosecution of small-time poachers. Three decades on, we might be less inclined to write off the rural poor as merely passive victims. Thomas Hardy cautioned a century ago against 'the error of supposing that actual slovenliness is always accompanied by unhappiness'. And a similar respect is at the heart of E. P. Thompson's classic, *The Making of the English Working Class* (1963), in which he declares his intention to rescue the creativity and resilience of the common people from the 'enormous condescension of posterity'. Edward Thompson was a radical, and might have frowned on his namesake's political naivety. But their approach to history was identical: a downplaying of the cold statistics of wages, living conditions and trade union structure in favour of the living details of what E. P. Thompson referred to as 'experience' – customs and rituals, reading clubs, popular songs, making do.

But English's point is a strong one, and needs an answer. If Flora was glossing over uncomfortable facts inside a framework which has all the appearance of a historical memoir, does that make her guilty of a kind of ruralist spin, of wilfully making village life appear more Arcadian than it was? It all depends, as you might expect, on what you mean by falsifying. Or, putting it another way, on the kinds of evidence Flora reckoned were not sacrosanct. She made her own position very clear in an extended subtitle to *Over to Candleford*. 'The following is intended less as autobiography than as a record of the impressions of a child brought up in a remote country hamlet, in the eighteen-eighties. It is written in the third person because the writer can best see objectively, across the gulf of time and war and change, the child who was herself moving in that now vanished world.' Despite such an explicit outlining of the book's imaginative base and sophisticated dual viewpoint, its superficial, yet artful simplicity meant it would continue to be read – and judged – as if it were a straightforward social documentary.

But what the young Flora was seeing and remembering – and the mature Flora reimagining as Laura's experience – was more nuanced: a framework of precisely recalled material details – words, foodstuffs, clothes, smells, the layout of rooms and the shadows under hedges – through which a cast of semi-fictionalized characters (including the author's young self) move, as in a novel. The novel has two sub-plots. One is the story of a young girl's growing-up and increasing self-awareness. The other, to use a phrase coined by the American writer Joseph W. Meeker, concerns 'the comedy of survival' of a poor but resourceful village community.

If, on the way, poverty, tragedy and sheer back-breaking toil are underplayed, then there is an implicit justification at the heart of Flora Thompson's books. She wanted to put on record the other, barely considered, side of the villagers' story: how they *handled* hardship, both as individuals and as a community. There are two stories of collective making-do in *Lark Rise* which, in their detail and contrasting pictures of where such survival tactics originate, counter the idea that Flora was simply intent on producing a sanitized, sentimental fantasy about a self-sufficient community 'where the sun shone all summer'.

The first story is one in which mutual aid is patrician in origin, but kept lively by grassroots input. After every new birth in the hamlet a small oak chest, universally known as 'THE BOX', made an appearance, usually lashed to the seat of one of the hamlet's two perambulators. The box was a local institution, a communal chest of baby-clothes, made, repaired and lent out by the Cottisford rector's daughter. It contained half a dozen of everything a newborn might need – tiny shirts, swathes, flannel 'barrows' (sleeveless infants' gowns), nighties and napkins. As a bonus, packets of tea and sugar and a tin of patent groats for making gruel were tucked in amongst the linen.

Any hamlet wife, regardless of whether she attended church, was welcome to borrow it. Like all benefits it began to be expected as a right, a 'provision of Nature', as Flora describes it, and was so constantly in demand that 'it had to have an understudy, known as "the second-best box", altogether inferior, which fell to the lot of those careless matrons who had neglected to bespeak the loan the moment they "knew their luck again"'. At the end of the month (though extensions were allowed) the mother would launder the clothes and return the box to the rectory, ready for the next arrival. This was charitableness working as a mixed economy.

The other story celebrates a fiercer kind of independence, and has an almost urban feel. One autumn evening in the mid-1880s, a cheap-jack makes his first appearance in the village and sets up his stall of mass-produced crockery and tinware on the grass, in front of a backcloth painted, improbably, with icebergs and penguins and polar bears. Flora catches expertly his non-stop patter of outrageous claims and nonsense rhymes. The hamlet audience, agog at this exotic intrusion by the modern world, are vastly entertained, but can't afford anything beyond penny nutmeg-graters and single plates.

Then the cheap-jack, badly needing a more substantial sale, produces his *pièce de résistance*, a twenty-one-piece tea-service, 'hand-painted' with pink roses, the twin, so he insists, of a set bought by the Queen. He wants twelve shillings for it, and taunts the villagers, asking them if they want Lark Rise to get the reputation of being 'the poverty-strickenist place on God's earth'. He passes the cups round the audience. They're handled longingly, but no one has the 'stockings from under the mattress' that the hawker is hoping for. Then an offer of ten bob is suddenly made from the back of the crowd. It's from a local man who has just returned from a spell of soldiering in India. 'All eyes were upon him. The credit of the hamlet was at stake.' They bargain briefly, and settle at eleven and six. After which the assembled Lark Risers help him carry the tea-service triumphantly home as if it were a collectively won football cup.

Doubtless Flora was selective in her anecdotes, and cherry-picked those which would serve as parables about the strength and inclusiveness of village mutuality. But the mundane particulars of the descriptions, the *stuff* of these social transactions, carry great conviction. Who would bother to invent such ordinary detailing? Gilbert White called such intimate witnesses 'nice' observers, meaning, strictly, sharp-eyed and discriminating, but also suggesting respect for what was observed.

10. Ballads and Bustles: Flora's folklore

Laura is made an especially 'nice' witness of folk-singing at the Lark Rise pub. But her exact recollections of performances and transcriptions of the songs raise more questions about the reliability of Flora's memories than any other part of the book – especially as (unknown to Laura but certainly not to Flora in the 1940s) the 1880s saw the beginning of the folk-song revival in Britain, and of an earnest intellectual debate about the identity of 'the Folk' and the nature of 'cultural authenticity'.

The men gathered at the Wagon and Horses ('The Fox' in Juniper Hill) every evening. It was, Flora insists (not entirely convincingly), an 'innocent gathering'. None of the men got drunk, their nightly intake being limited to half a pint by the weekly allowance of a shilling doled out by their wives. But they sang, and Flora faithfully reproduces the words of their songs. How she was able to do this is a little perplexing. Women and children didn't go inside the pub, by long tradition. The hamlet kids lurked outside the door, or perched on the stairs with the landlord's children, soaking up political gossip, tall stories, and the nightly procession of 1880s pop songs, medieval ballads and daft agricultural work-ditties.

The programme was never the same, but always started with the young men, who had 'first innings' with the music-hall songs that had percolated as far as the hamlet. 'Over the Garden Wall' and 'Two Lovely Black Eyes' were already perennial favourites. Lukey, the hamlet's only bachelor of a mature age, gave his self-teasing version of 'They say I shall die an old maid' ('There's nobody coming to marry/And there's nobody coming to woo'). But the older men preferred more mournful songs, ballads about thwarted love and lost children, especially Master Price's tear-jerking version of 'Lord Lovell', sung while he supported himself with the stick he called his third leg:

> And they buried her in the chancel high,
>   And they buried him in the choir;
> And out of her grave sprung a red, red rose,
>   And out of his sprung a briar.
>
> And they grew till they grew to the church roof,
>   And then they couldn't grow any higher;
> So they twined themselves in a true lovers' knot,
>   For all lovers true to admire.

Flora remarks that the men were always quiet and reflective after this song, saddened both by its content and Master Price's frailty. The evening usually ended with a call for 'old David's' version of the classic 'Outlandish Knight', 'not because they wanted particularly to hear it – indeed, they had heard it so often they all knew it by heart – but because, as they said, "Poor old feller be eighty-three. Let 'un sing while he can."' Also because it was his special and only song, passed down through at least four generations of his family; and because its tale of an elvish serial killer who is tricked and drowned by his next hoped-for victim doubtless had the power to send shivers through nineteenth-century audiences just as it has in the twenty-first century.

Flora quotes eleven stanzas of this epic ballad. Even with her almost eidetic memory it's unlikely that she had flawless recall of every lyric. She may have made transcriptions in a

child's notebook, now lost. But it's more plausible that, in the
1940s, she used published versions of this and the other ballads quoted in *Lark Rise* to prompt her memory.

The first printed version of 'The Outlandish Knight'
appeared in Herd's collection of Scottish songs in 1776. It
became more widely available with the publication of the
'Child Ballads' between 1882 and 1898. Francis Child was a
Harvard scholar who made an exhaustive collection of traditional English folk songs and ballads, working entirely from
manuscript and printed sources. His published version of
'The Outlandish Knight' is similar – and in a few verses virtu-
ally identical – to the one quoted by Flora. But in the early
1940s she would have been able to see many more variants, in
popular books of songs for schools and choirs, for instance,
the consequence of a movement that had started sixty years
previously. It was one of those moments of synchronicity
that seem to occur throughout Flora's life. While she was
sitting outside the Fox, straining her young ears to catch
the words of these ancient stories of honour and betrayal,
more grown-up and purposeful listeners elsewhere in Britain
were doing precisely the same, and starting a process that
would transform the public awareness of home-grown folk
music.

The 'Folk Revival' was one of the early manifestations of the
idea of going 'back to the land', the 'flight to the rural' that
began in the mid nineteenth century, and which has pulsed
intermittently ever since. Along with a blossoming interest in
country traditions, arts and crafts, natural history and community living (all of which are celebrated in Thompson's own
books), the Revival can be seen as a reaction to develop-
ments in an increasingly urban and industrialized Britain.

Concerned observers from the puritan wing of the intelligent-sia saw a culture in collapse in Victorian Britain. The people (once 'the Folk') were swarming into the cities, living in squalor and moral decay. They had abandoned their old skills and their inherited good taste. Their liking for vulgar songs from music-halls and street-singers was a demonstration of just how far they had degenerated.

Sir Hubert Parry, composer of 'Jerusalem' and later Professor of Music at Oxford, used his inaugural address to the newly formed Folk-Song Society in 1898 to express a mis-anthropic contempt for the whole culture he and others believed was suffocating Old England. 'If one thinks of the outer circumference of our terribly overgrown towns, where the jerry-builder holds sway, where one sees all around the tawdriness of sham jewellery and shoddy clothes, pawn-shops and flaming gin-palaces . . . all such things suggest to one's mind the boundless regions of sham. It is for the people who live in these unhealthy regions – people who, for the most part, have the most false ideals, or none at all, who are always struggling for existence, who think that the common-est rowdyism is the highest expression of human emotion; it is for them that modern popular music is made . . . And this product it is which will drive out folk music if we do not save it . . . old folk-music is among the purest products of the human mind. It grew in the hearts of the people before they devoted themselves so assiduously to the making of quick returns.' This latter 'product', it hardly needs adding, was to be found at its purest and most authentic in rural villages as yet uncorrupted by urban vulgarity.

The Revival had begun in Britain in the 1840s, with the Revd John Broadwood, who collected Christmas songs in the Weald of

Sussex and Surrey. During the 1880s Broadwood's niece Lucy continued his work, and the Revd Sabine Baring-Gould (mostly famous for his hymns) began collecting in Devon. To begin with the motivation for their work was antiquarian, to save fascinating fragments of vernacular culture from likely extinction. But unlike Francis Child in America, they believed that the content and spirit of what was essentially an oral form couldn't be captured from written texts. So they edged their way into pubs and village backrooms with their notebooks and sheets of manuscript paper and jotted down the songs as they were sung, *in situ*.

The idea that this provided a direct line to 'authenticity' was of course naive in the extreme. The antics of this generation of field collectors – bribing farm-workers to sing, hiding in cupboards to 'overhear' more personal ditties, sometimes editing out material they found unsavoury or which failed to fit their assumptions about what constituted 'pure' folk music – read more like the behaviour of social security snoops than that of scholarly folklorists. And their concentration on live performance was, in practice, contradictory. Instead of valuing the diverse personalities and interpretations of the singers (the agents who, after all, had kept the folk tradition alive), the early collectors paid chief attention to the *songs*, which they regarded as musical fossils, relics of a vanished peasant or even 'savage' musical culture. Individual performers were simply channelling, and often 'degrading', these ancient archetypes.

A semi-mystical belief in 'the Folk', a kind of proto-community from which song and dance, and for that matter stories, craft-skills, farming ways and children's games, emerged by some mysterious process that bypassed the creativity of individuals, bedevilled thinking about rural life well into the twentieth century. (Though Flora remained mercifully unimpressed by or uninterested in this ideology. Despite having experienced its influence at close quarters – for example at Grayshott – she remained throughout her writing life committed to real individuals, not symbols or archetypes.) At a time when so much in Britain – class hierarchies, the role of women, even the look of the landscape – was in a state of flux, the idea that there was an untainted well of national music, just waiting for discovery and dissemination, was seductive. Among the more idealistic it raised the possibility that folk music could become a focus for the salvation of a unified 'Merrie England'.

But untaintedness was the key. Songs or individual performances which diverged from the ideal form, which were too idiosyncratic, which showed signs of corruption by modern influences, were not products of 'the Folk' at all.* So the Revival needed gatekeepers and curators, self-appointed arbiters of taste, who could discriminate between true roots music and cheapened derivatives. By a bizarre circular argument, the 'Folk' themselves couldn't fulfil this role, because as soon as they became consciously self-critical, they ceased to have the primitive purity which qualified them to be members of the tribe, to be 'Folk'.

The new and well-connected English Folk Dance Society, under the autocratic leadership of Cecil Sharp, was happy to play this paternal role in their place. Sharp, a professional

* Georgina Boyes, whose book *The Imagined Village* (1993) is a scholarly and bracing exposure of the cultural paternalism and internal power struggles of the Folk Revival, quotes a telling story by the nineteenth-century collector Anne Gilchrist about the singer William Bolton: 'Having a chantyman's gift for verse-making, he had himself supplied words for a hiatus between verses one and two in the shanty "Rounding Cape Horn". But as his own verses were less artless than the remainder of this genuine if doggerel production of some sailor bard, I have omitted them in order to maintain its character.'

music teacher and amateur folklorist, was credited (falsely) with conjuring the Revival into existence in 1903 when he happened to hear and be lifted by John England singing 'The Seeds of Love' in a Somerset vicarage garden. But he took on the nascent Society with a missionary zeal, and for the next two decades set the rules about how songs should be recorded, preserved and, especially, spread about, because a folk-music revival was nothing if it did not reach out to the nation. So, ragged, sometimes off-tone renderings were spruced up into tonic sol-fa notation. Bawdiness and the more blatant *double entendres* were struck out. Song books with easy piano accompaniments were mass-printed for use in schools.

Sharp rejected charges by dissenters in the Revival movement that he was taking a too purist and authoritarian line and failing to catch the populist and evolving spirit of real folk music. The Revival was not a cult, he protested, 'appropriated and patronized by a few choice spirits and protected from the common herd. Whereas it was the common herd . . . to which [the music] belonged; and to whom it was my intention to restore their lost heritage.'

There are clear echoes here of the debate about pastoral literature, and whether authentic 'renderings' of grass-roots rural life could ever be created by people who were not intrinsically part of that life. As usual, Flora, the class border-hopper, cannot be shoehorned into any orthodox position in the argument. She quite likely used transcriptions by Sharp's disciples for the folk-song lyrics in *Lark Rise*, though none of the purist thinking that underlay them. She names the singers and personalizes their performances with her asides about their style and habits. She relishes the way the young men turned songs from the 'outer world' into a kind of modern folk music, bawling out music-hall favourites with 'good lusty voices'.

In one instance she becomes an original – and liberal-minded – collector herself, registering a song which certainly did not figure in any of the approved songbooks, a verse by a homesick incomer from Deddington, a village about six miles west of Juniper Hill. It is pure doggerel and has a doubtful last line (the pub name in the original must have been the less metric 'the Fox') but it belonged uniquely to the singer:

> Where be Dedington boo-oys, where be they now?
> They be at Dedington at the 'Plough';
> If they be-ent, they be at home,
> And this is the 'Wagon and Horses'.

There is just one false note in Flora's account of the pub-singing session. Flora, standing back from her exact memories, reflects that: 'The singers were rude and untaught and poor beyond modern imagining; but they deserve to be remembered, for they knew the now lost secret of being happy on little' – which sounds an overly simplistic version of what she has just described.

I'm more taken by the vivid image she has conjured up of these evening song sessions: the men, spending the pocket-money allowed them by their wives and chanting ballads about courtly ladies; the real women back at home, doubtless regaling each other with far more bawdy tales; and between them this young girl, Laura, the listener and 'remembrancer', soaking up every detail as her own cultural capital. It's a vivid reminder that *Lark Rise* is principally a tribute to rural *women* (so often absent from orthodox social history) and what they were capable of.

As Flora puts it: 'The men worked for the money and the women had the spending of it. The men had the best of the bargain. They earned their half-sovereign by hard toil, it is true, but in the open air, at work they liked and took an interest in, and in congenial company. The women, kept close at home, with cooking, cleaning, washing, and mending to do, plus their constant pregnancies and a tribe of children to look after, had also the worry of ways and means on an insufficient income.' Flora escaped most of these worries by leaving the hamlet. But she had absorbed the energy of these resourceful women, and her own life was also to become a story of finding 'ways and means' against the odds.

*

The critic Juliet Dusinberre has suggested how the power of *Lark Rise* comes from an interweaving of an essentially child-like *vision* with an adult *voice*. 'Thompson records a past which is still vividly present in her consciousness, refusing to accept change at the core of her own identity. But the voice which acknowledges the power of memory to recreate and relive the experience of the child is that of the adult who apprehends a changing world.'

Of course, the child's first impression and the adult's re-telling regularly clash, as well as refracting each other. One of Laura's favourite stories concerned a little girl who found a concealed opening on the heath, which led to an underground palace in which all the furniture and hangings were pale blue and silver. The heroine's adventures left no impression on Laura, while the blue and silver under the earth left an afterglow in her imagination. Laura begged her mother to re-tell the story, but the magic was never the same. The disappointment became as vivid a part of her memory as the sensual details of the story. Laura had come up against the treachery of remembered details, and their tantalizing power to recreate an experience without always summoning up the emotions originally attached to it.*

Of all the physical details of her life that young Laura registered, none are remembered more vividly and meaningfully by Flora than the ways people – herself included – dressed. Her observations of clothing are among the sharpest passages of her writing and make a vivid and witty commentary on the social sensitivities of her fellow villagers, and her own strategies for relating to them.

Comments on dress, like graphic captions, occur throughout *Lark Rise to Candleford* – an inadvertent glimpse of a severe aunt's purple petticoat, a pregnancy disguised by a crinoline, the village boys' fondness for donning bows and ribbons on May Day – though they have been largely ignored by writers on Flora Thompson, perhaps believing that to highlight Flora's fascination with dress might cast her as a female stereotype, or undermine her lyrical and historical seriousness. Exactly the opposite seems to be true. Flora's fashion notes celebrate the enduring inventiveness of rural women and are among the most creative and empathetic passages in her books. And as the novelist Elizabeth Bowen suggested, dress as a topic is

* In an essay on *Alice in Wonderland* in his book *Some Versions of the Pastoral* (1960), William Empson argues that a child's world, with its innocence and magical visions, can itself be a kind of 'pastoral' retreat every bit as seductive and sedative as an idyllic countryside from the past.

inherently fascinating, 'because it is dangerous – it has a flow-ery head but deep roots in the passions'.

Flora confessed late in her life that she had always found dif-ficulty in accessing passion's deep roots, and in finding ways of expressing the 'inner emotions . . . for I have led an isolated life mentally and spiritually'. This 'difficulty', combined with an almost obsessive attention to and memory for surface details, might, in these reductionist times, be seen as evidence that Flora had a psychological 'problem'. But I don't think there was anything disturbed or socially evasive in Flora's personal-ity and behaviour. Rather, she used her understanding of and receptiveness to dress as a way of getting closer to people, not of avoiding them.

Flora provides an early introduction to the significance of appearances. The young Laura is regarded as distinctly 'odd' by the hamlet, and is nicknamed a 'werrit' (an annoying nosy parker). The villagers, eyeing her gawky plainness, pronounce that she was 'Like a moll heron, all legs and wings', adding for good measure that she was 'cross-grained', on account of her unusual mix of blonde hair and dark eyes. The only compli-ment ever paid to her appearance during childhood was by the curate, who thought she was 'intelligent looking'. 'Those around her', Flora remarks ruefully, 'would have preferred curly hair and a rosebud mouth to all the intelligence in the world.'

'[N]ever you mind, my poppet', the neighbours say to her. 'Good looks ain't everything, and you can't help it if you did hap-pen to be behind the door when they were being given out.' Her mother tries to help by sprucing up her daughter's hand-me-down wardrobe with a little fancy sewing, but Laura is teased so much by the other children about the lace on her drawers that once she took them off and hid them in a haystack. It was a temporary setback. From then on, right into her mature years, Laura uses dress as a way of asserting her personality, of standing out from the crowd (or losing herself in it where necessary), and of providing sheer, self-indulgent pleasure.

Writing forty years later in *Heatherley*, Flora (by then well read in Freud and Henry James) hints that her childhood was 'restricted'. There's little evidence of this in anything else she wrote about her early years, and by today's standards she grew up in an environment of extraordinary freedom. Her father may have had bouts of bad temper, and her mother of brusque, albeit affectionate, insensitivity. But Flora was a long way from being repressed or confined. If, with hindsight, she felt she was 'restricted', it was more a consequence of her social awkwardness and highly strung emotions than any deliberate subjugation by her parents. And these were aspects of her personality that, from her earliest years, she compensated for by dressing up.

When Laura is aged about thirteen, she accompanies a friend to an interview for a maid's job. She tricks herself out in an outrageous outfit – chimney-pot hat, short brown cape, buttoned boots reaching nearly her knees – that is absolutely a teenager on an adult outing. (Though she wasn't always able to erase the village's image of her as a cumbersome crane-fly. When fashion in the outside world was beginning to favour short frocks for small girls, Laura acquired from one of her town cousins a knee-length cream frock with red polka dots, which her mother had highlighted with a red hair-ribbon. Her chic outfit, alas, was too advanced for the hamlet children on their riotous journey to school. They yelled abuse at her exposed and spindly legs – 'Hamfrill!', 'Longshanks!' – questioned her mother's respectability, and then rolled her over in the dust.)

Flora understood the ways in which her fellow villagers used dress, too, as a gesture of defiance against the drabness of their workaday lives, and a medium through which they could express their aspirations and social positions. Their low incomes meant that they had to work with mediocre stock, second-hand bits sent home by daughters in service and utility garments made from material donated by the rectory – chemises of unbleached calico, flannel petticoats, worsted stockings. But the women loved 'anything a bit dressy', and dyed and patched this rough stuff until they had something with a modicum of appeal. For all except the very aged women, dressing as best you could was a matter of self-respect and community pride. 'Better be out of the world than out of the fashion' was a popular local saw – though Flora reckoned that it took one or two years for a fashion from the outside world to penetrate as far as the hamlet.

When it did arrive it still had to be adapted to local custom and prejudice. A red frock? 'Only a fast hussy would wear red. Or green – sure to bring any wearer bad luck!' The onset of the bustle was a major event. These extraordinary conceits first became popular in English fashion as a reaction against the cumbersome vastness of the crinoline, in the 1840s. They died out in the 1870s, only to return again as the defining feature of late Victorian fashion. They signalled modesty and curvaceous mystery at the same time.

When bustles first hit Lark Rise, they were looked on with horror, 'but after a year or two [became] the most popular fashion ever known in the hamlet and the one which lasted longest. They cost nothing, as they could be made at home from any piece of old cloth rolled up into a cushion and worn under any frock. Soon all the women, excepting the aged, and all the girls, excepting the tiniest, were peacocking in their bustles, and they wore them so long that Edmund was old enough in the day of their decline to say that he had seen the last bustle on earth going round the Rise on a woman with a bucket of pig-wash.'*

Flora also understood that fashion was a prism for the inflections of class, and sometimes an expression of a feisty pride in one's status, however marginal. She describes the functional clothes of the half-dozen women who still did part-time field-work in Lark Rise in the 1880s, earning four shillings a week for a six-hour shift. They worked in sun-bonnets, hobnailed boots and men's coats. One, Mrs Spicer, was a pioneer in the wearing of trousers and sported a pair of her husband's corduroys. The others compromised with the ends of old trouser legs worn as gaiters. The gentry flitted past such rustic scenes 'like king-fishers crossing a flock of hedgerow sparrows'. Flora catches the details of their self-presentation so tellingly: 'the ladies billowing in silk and satins, with tiny chenille-fringed parasols held at an angle to protect their complexions.'

But it is dress as a badge of personal identity and stubborn idiosyncrasy that she understands best. Her note on Lark Rise's dutiful postman is as deft as a cartoon: 'On wet days he carried an old green gig umbrella with whalebone ribs, and, beneath its immense circumference he seemed to make no more progress than an overgrown mushroom.' As is her aside on the butcher who had slaughtered their pig, and 'draped a long, lacy piece of fat from its own interior over one of its forelegs, in the manner in which ladies of that day sometimes

* 'For Queen Victoria's Golden Jubilee celebrations, a patriotic inventor patented a bustle containing a musical box which played "God Save the Queen" whenever the wearer sat down – an exhausting device, for naturally she had immediately to rise again, and everyone else with her!' Alison Gernsheim, *Victorian and Edwardian Fashion* (1981).

carried a white lacy shawl' – a touch which seemed utterly heartless to Laura, but whose meaning Flora had no problem reading.

11.   *War Work: the launching of the trilogy*

In the summer of 1938, Thompson was able to put together fifteen potential chapters of *Lark Rise* and send them off to Oxford University Press. Why she chose OUP isn't clear. There was no Ronald Macfie figure to intercede on her behalf, nor did the university press have a reputation for handling rural memoirs.

Perhaps the sign by the turnpike at Juniper Hill – OXFORD XIX MILES – and the intangible allure of that distant city still held a spell over her. Whatever the reason, her manuscript ended up, providentially, on the desk of the Publisher to the University, Sir Humphrey Milford, who since his appointment in 1913 had moved the Press in a more populist direction. He encouraged Flora to expand her essays into a full-length book, and suggested that she should be edited by his deputy, Geoffrey Cumberlege (later to succeed Milford as Publisher).

But there was a snag. Flora wanted her book classified as a novel but OUP didn't publish fiction at the time. So Cumberlege had it labelled as autobiography – a branding which has affected the perception of Flora's books ever since, irritating pedantic critics, misleading historians and maybe losing her some of the serious literary appreciation and analysis she craved.

Over the summer, Lynton Lamb, who had trained at the Central School of Arts and Crafts and was a staff illustrator for OUP, prepared the illustrations for the book. He based himself at the Crown Hotel in Brackley, meandered around Juniper

Hill for a few days, and ended up with ten pen and ink draw-ings. They included the thatched cottage where Flora was born (demolished just after the war) and a beguilingly impressionist sketch of two bicycles leaning against a tumbledown barn, cap-tioned by a line from the text: 'games were played in the open spaces between the cottages'.

In February 1939, Geoffrey Cumberlege told Flora that there was interest in her book in America. He had forwarded her early chapters to OUP's New York office and had received an enthusiastic note from the managing editor, who knew noth-ing of Flora's long and difficult apprenticeship: 'I have been reading with a great feeling of contentment the instalments of *Lark Rise* which have been turning up. I like it and am terri-bly glad to turn to it in spare moments. It has an amazing English quality of permanence and repose. I should very much like to know the history of the author. She writes with such ease that it is hard to believe she has not considerable literary experience.'

What probably sealed the publication date for *Lark Rise* was the imminence of war. In March 1939, as Hitler marched on Prague and Franco swaggered over the Republican white flag in Madrid, Flora Thompson's folk-tale was published, and a nerv-ous Britain welcomed its stories of communal resilience and ancient values. *Punch*, *The Times*, the *Yorkshire Post* and *Country Life* all praised it. Flora was gratified, as were OUP, and she was given the go-ahead for the sequel she had planned from the outset. The declaration of war in September wasn't un-expected, but it brought practical difficulties for Flora as well as the anxieties she shared with everyone else in the nation, espe-cially the mothers. Her son Peter went to work in Dartmouth's shipyards, a prime target for any bombing raids. John worked all day on air-raid precaution work. The blackout was strictly enforced in the town, and Flora spent a whole week making curtains from Peter's old camping blankets.

She was sixty-four years old and her health was deteriorating, but she soldiered on with what she had already entitled *Over to Candleford*. Geoffrey Cumberlege offered what encouragement he could: 'We all hope you will push on with it as hard as you can and let us have it as soon as possible.' But Dartmouth was looking increasingly vulnerable, and John and Flora decided to look for a safer place to live. Then, in November 1939, their son Peter enlisted in the merchant navy, making any hope of a family refuge futile.

Flora was by now finding it almost impossible to work on her new typescript and in January 1940 wrote to Cumberlege offering to repay her advance. He replied with characteristic calming support: 'Write the book in your own time, it will always be welcome here and you are still extremely welcome to the advance that has been paid to you. No promise has been broken because the war has upset everybody's calculations.' John was also providing his wife with an unprecedented level of support. He bought home fresh-caught fish and cooked their supper while Flora laboured at the Remington.

By March 1940 they had found a house in Brixham, on the coast four miles to the north. It was a substantial old cottage built into a hillside and hidden from the sea and the town centre. Lauriston (was its name a coincidence, or did Flora name it herself in honour of her newly dubbed childhood self?) was spacious enough to have a spare room, which Flora converted into a study. It also had a very large cellar, in which the Thompsons installed the government-issue metal caging known as the 'Morrison shelter'. They had to use it during the latter part of 1940, when south Devon began to suffer air attacks from the newly occupied French coast. But Flora succeeded in finishing *Over to Candleford* late that year, and it was published in the spring of 1941.

The odd thing about the text is that not a hint of the tribulations against which it was written – a world war, bombing raids, social upheaval – seeps into the mood of its prose, except by offering up a defiant contrast to them. Flora, perhaps conscious of this, doubted the book's value, and worried that she had produced something lightweight and inappropriate. The press and public disagreed, and *Over to Candleford* received, if anything, even more acclaim than *Lark Rise*. May 1941 saw the darkest days of the Blitz in London, and Athens fell to the Germans. But Flora's growing company of followers seemed keen to forget the war and learn what happened next to Laura, and Cumberlege urged Flora on, despite her diffidence and mediocre health: 'If you have another book in you don't hesitate to start getting it out of your system and on to paper.'

On 16 September 1941, the Thompsons received a telegram informing them that their son's ship, the *Jedmoor*, carrying a cargo of wheat, had been torpedoed. Only six of the crew had been saved and Peter was not one of them. Flora revealed little in print about her feelings for her children, and seemed to take the heartbreaking news stoically. She wrote to Cumberlege saying 'that there are thousands of mothers and wives suffering as I am only seems to make it harder to bear'; and later to her friend Arthur Ball that 'the world is in such a state today that sometimes I feel that he, being at rest, is better off than those still at sea'. Her friend and colleague Mildred Humble-Smith also lost a son at sea, and the two bereaved mothers decided to disband the Peverel Society immediately.

Flora buried her sorrow in work. For her next book she was outlining a piece of straight fiction, the story of a house called

Dashpers, and the people who lived in it. She sent a précis and a sample chapter to Cumberlege, who responded by saying, 'I am sure we shall like it although it will, of course, be rather different from the other two.' This was too hesitant for Flora's frayed nerves and melancholy mood and she abandoned the idea.

That winter she contracted pneumonia and was in her sickbed for weeks. She never fully recovered, but in the spring of 1942 began work on a sequel to her Lark Rise and Candleford books, to be entitled *Candleford Green*. The writing became an endurance test. Dartmouth was suffering repeated bombing raids. The Royal Naval College and the shipyard where Peter had worked were both badly hit, with heavy loss of life. Even Brixham came under attack, too, as hit-and-run raiders offloaded their bombs onto the docks. In one of the few of her private letters to survive, Flora wrote to her friend Anna Ball about her daily treks with the big Remington typewriter every time the sirens sounded: 'I have almost finished my new book *Candleford Green*. It has been written under difficulties, several passages to the sound of bombs falling and the typescript already looks worn through being taken in and out of the Morrison shelter.'

Candleford Green was finally published in January 1943. Its story, centred on resourceful women like Dorcas Lane, Mrs Macey and indeed Laura herself, sounded a chord on the Home Front, and the book was another success. The *Times Literary Supplement* commented that 'Miss Thompson's readers have coalesced into a faithful band of followers of what promises to be an unusual series; we wait, impatient for the next instalment.' But one review, in *Time and Tide*, sounded a more portentous note: 'In her shell we hear the thunder of an ocean of change, a change tragic indeed, since nothing has taken and nothing can take the place of what has gone. A design for living has become unravelled.'

This sounded not at all like the inventive and adaptable society Flora had documented. But the review was by H. J. Massingham and was therefore taken note of; and as OUP made preparations to publish all three titles as a single volume in 1944, Cumberlege invited Massingham to write what would become a keynote introduction, whose ripples have still not entirely died away. He accepted, and Flora wrote to him flushed with demure pride: 'I feel I must tell you what a very great pleasure this good news has given me. I feel honoured that you should be willing to stand godfather to my simple records, and I am pleased and relieved to know that my offspring is now assured of kind and sympathetic treatment.'

Seventy years on Massingham seems an odd choice of 'godfather'. He had certainly established himself as a knowledgeable and intellectually original commentator on countryside matters in the 1920s and 1930s. By the outbreak of war he had published more than twenty books that ranged, polymathically, over topography, rural crafts, natural history and archaeology. As a kind of indigenous anthropologist he made invaluable records of a changing physical and social landscape and posted some of the first ecological concerns about what was happening to the farming countryside.

But he differed radically from Flora in two significant ways. First, he was an ideologue, with set beliefs about how rural society had worked and should work. In place of the tangy and contrary lives of real country people, he set down abstracted stereotypes of 'the peasant' and 'the countryman', miming their roles in some immemorial 'organic society'. His observations had always to fit into his theories, with sometimes laughable results (e.g. eighteenth-century land-scapers' conceits interpreted as mystical Celtic ciphers). Second, he was an aggressive pessimist, who believed that the only redemption for industrialized humanity lay in the return to a peasant society.

In this he differed even from other gloomily inclined rural commentators. Richard Jefferies had declared that his 'sympathies and hopes are with the light of the future', and wanted, in his biographer Edward Thomas's wonderfully exact phrase, 'the light railway to call at the farmyard gate'. George Sturt, in some ways the thinker whose ideas were closest to Massingham's, stated his similar position unambiguously: 'I would not go back. I would not lift a finger, or say a word, to restore the past time, for fear lest in doing so I might be retarding a movement which, when I can put these sentiments aside, looks like a renaissance of the English country-folk.'* Flora – who applauded the arrival of the old-age pension and improvements in villagers' welfare, and celebrated the tenacious quirkiness of her Oxfordshire compatriots rather than lamenting their supposed destruction – agreed, and insisted that, 'For myself, I would desire a combination of old romance and modern machinery'.

It would be wrong to overestimate the influence of Massingham's introduction. But it has stuck to Flora's text like a jarring graffito and acted as an easy target for later critics who wish to

---

* Yet the critics F. R. Leavis and Denys Thompson, in their polemical book *Culture and Environment* (1933), thought they saw quite different sentiments in Sturt's work: that far from there being a renaissance in 'the English country-folk', they and their 'organic community' had been destroyed by mass culture and their only hope of redemption lay in a return to the patterns of life and work of 'the past time'.

brand *Lark Rise to Candleford* as nothing more than nostalgic Luddism. Massingham describes Thompson's books (in which, incidentally, he sees the only actors as 'country*men*' (my italics)) as being the story of 'the utter ruin of a closely knit organic society with a richly interwoven and traditional culture', and stresses that Flora Thompson 'makes us see the passing of this England, not as a milestone along the road of inevitable progress, but as the attempted murder of something timeless in and quintessential to the spirit of man'.

Massingham's thunderous prose reads now like a self-parody, but at the time Flora was flattered that this starry figure from the English literary establishment was to be at the forefront of her book, and she wrote again to thank him for his words: 'Words as to inner emotions do not come readily to me, for I have led an isolated life mentally and spiritually . . . The very few people I know personally . . . are not reading people, and though reviewers have been kind and I have had a few letters of appreciation from readers, no one but you has recognized my aims and intentions in writing of that more excellent way of life of our forefathers.' Massingham was twelve years younger than Flora, so was not another 'older man'. But he had the kind of standing and aura that Flora had always been impressed by, and which, despite the success of her books, she was no closer to achieving herself.

The three books were published in a combined edition in March 1945, and the inspired title *Lark Rise to Candleford* helped it to an even warmer critical reception. But apart from her meagre royalties, Flora hardly benefited. Even after the war ended in May 1945 there was no literary feting in London, no invitations to give talks or broadcasts. She was commissioned to review Alison Uttley's *Country Hoard* in the

Listener and that was all. It was as if the literary establishment preferred to keep her at a safe distance and maintain the myth of the 'Village Postmistress Poetess', rather than risk the revelations (or embarrassments) that might come with the public presentation of a real, self-made, working-class woman writer. No wonder that when Flora was encouraged to produce yet another book she seemed to have no real heart for it.

She had already offered to finish *Dashpers*, but Cumberlege had discouraged her: 'I like everything you write, but I do not think this shows you at your happiest.' Next Flora had sent him a clutch of 'Peverel Papers', and a proposal to make an anthology from them. This met with a more positive response from OUP, yet for some reason Flora didn't persist with the idea and it would be more than thirty years before the articles appeared in book form. While she was waiting for the publication of the *Lark Rise to Candleford* trilogy, she wrote her sequel, *Heatherley*, but never submitted it to OUP. Perhaps, even with the editing she had done, she felt it too revealing of her behaviour as a grown woman, for whom the 'child's eye' of Laura was not really appropriate.

Her last resort, as it seemed to have been throughout her life, was to retreat to fiction. In the summer of 1945, she began writing an undisguised novel, called initially *These Too Were Victorians* (eventually to become *Still Glides the Stream*). It would be set, like *Lark Rise*, in the Oxfordshire countryside of the 1880s, but instead of the partly real Laura, the central character would be entirely fictional, a retired schoolteacher called Charity Finch, who revisits the scenes of her childhood. Geoffrey Cumberlege liked the sample she sent him: 'I have been spending a delightful evening with the first chapter. We all like Charity Finch both in name and character and Clerk Savings is another inspiration. It all rings true and if you keep it up to this level, as you will, you need have no fear that you will not satisfy your devotees. I congratulate you.' He backed up his approval with an advance of £50 and free typing paper, which was in short supply after the war.

Cumberlege may have been acting more from kindness than real editorial conviction. Flora was now chronically ill, affected by increasingly severe attacks of angina, and languishing in the severe winter of 1945–6. She wrote to a friend that she would love to see Dartmoor again, but that it would have to be from a bus, with two hot-water bottles, two fur coats and fur leggings: 'That's what I have come to . . . There was a time when I should have loved to face the cold and wind alone in one of the most inaccessible spots.'

When the typescript of *These Too Were Victorians* was delivered in August 1946, Cumberlege hedged his response. He said that he enjoyed it, but was worried about the ponderous and dated title. Within a couple of weeks Flora had changed it to a phrase borrowed from Wordsworth's sonnet to the 'River Duddon' – 'Still glides the Stream'. Cumberlege preferred this, but still prevaricated, saying now that the book couldn't be published immediately. After Flora's death he admitted he had reservations about the book and wondered if he had exerted too much pressure on a sick woman simply to produce some sequel to what was proving, for OUP, a bestseller.

His later judgement was the right one. *Still Glides the Stream* is an inconsequential book, remote, prim, with barely realized characters and no plot to speak of. *Lark Rise* sang because Flora had inhabited it both in real life and in her imagination. *Still Glides the Stream* was no more than dutifully written out, a long version of her journeywoman short stories of the 1920s.

★

In the end Flora was not to see its publication in 1948. She had one more moment of glory when Sir Humphrey Milford was interviewed in April 1946 for OUP's house magazine, *The Periodical*, and was asked which he considered the two most important books the Press had brought out during his thirty-two years as university publisher. He chose Arnold Toynbee's *A Study of History* and *Lark Rise to Candleford*, and added that both dealt in 'the history behind history', and both had the rare ability to enlighten, entrance and excite at the same time.

The winter of 1946–7 was the worst for more than a century. The blizzards began on 20 January and snow fell somewhere in Britain every day for two months. When the thaw began on 16 March, there were terrible floods, including across the West Country. Flora described the conditions in Brixham in a letter to a friend: 'The road outside our gate was a raging torrent like a river in spate. At the town end of the road the houses were flooded on the ground floors, the Post Office and most of the shops were awash and people in the lower part of the town had to be rescued from their upper windows by men in boats. Our cellar was flooded and we were without gas for twenty-four hours.' Flora was ill again during the bad weather, but seemed to recover with the return of warm weather in May, and on the 21st John felt she was well enough to leave in the house while he went out on business. When he came home in the evening he found her back in bed, having had a severe angina attack at midday. She died that night of a heart attack, aged seventy.

12. Celebrating England

But Flora Thompson's books had gained a life of their own. The idea that Britain is essentially a rural nation, and the countryside a metaphorical fortress of our way of life and values – always a mainstay of indigenous literature – had flourished strongly during the war and was actively encouraged in government propaganda. In 1942 Laurie Lee was commissioned to write lyrical articles about the English landscape and his young years in the Cotswolds (they became the germ for another classic account of a country childhood, *Cider with Rosie*).

The Crown Film Unit organized 25,000 showings of wartime documentaries around the country, including films such as Humphrey Jennings's* *Christmas Under Fire*, which cut between a blitzed London and an embedded rural village ('Today in England even the shepherds are in some kind of uniform', ran one line in the commentary). And J. B. Priestley's chummy Sunday broadcasts rambled across southern England's 'round green hills dissolving into the hazy blue sky' rather more than they did through the embattled industrial cities of his native north.

Late in the spring of 1942, the Ministry of Information featured a similar, half-mythic summer landscape in a series of

* Jennings's book *Pandæmonium 1660–1886: The Coming of the Machine as Seen by Contemporary Observers* (1985) was the principal inspiration for Danny Boyle's 2012 Olympic extravaganza and its inclusive vision of English history, in which the pre-industrial scenes, with their maypole-dancing and village cricket, could have come straight out of *Lark Rise*.

posters, resonantly entitled 'Your Britain – Fight for it Now'. The artist was Frank Newbould, born, like Priestley, in urban Bradford and trained at Camberwell School of Art in south London. He had chosen four scenes, all of them rural, and all of them, despite the campaign's title, located in the south country: a great oak on a village green, the raw material of the 'wooden walls' that had defended the country from attack three centuries before; Salisbury Cathedral, glimpsed through the trees, much as it had been by John Constable; a fair in the Sussex village of Alfriston, with a Union Jack waving from the top of a roundabout; and Sussex again for what has become one of the most enduring images from the war years. *The South Downs* is a masterly, manipulative picture, which melds together ancient, heart-tugging emblems of home and security with an unquestioning insistence that the nation, the 'country', can be identified with its 'countryside'.

The view is from the top of a hill looking down towards a sheltered valley. Nestling in the coombe, and surrounded by a billowing crescent of trees, is the picture's focal point, a large, red-roofed, doubled-chimneyed Tudor farmhouse. It glows with intimations of warmth and protective history, and we know that if we could look inside there would be a half-timbered kitchen and Sussex shirehorse-brasses hanging around an open hearth. Outside a shepherd is leading his flock back down to the farm. In the distance there are more 'round green hills dissolving into the hazy blue sky', and just glimpsed through a gap in the hills, the English Channel, the last ditch between us and the enemy. The scene is a tone-perfect portrait of what is sometimes called 'Deep England', an idealized, lost domain which is turned to yearningly every time the country is in trouble.

Flora Thompson had lived on the edge of the Channel herself, in Brixham, and a sense of being on the front line can't have failed to influence the gravity of her work. She had her own agenda, but she was working on essentially the same kind of project as Frank Newbould, tapping cultural history in a way that would lift the people's morale and remind them of their origins. But Flora wasn't offering an escape route into some sentimentalized version of the past. Even the physical setting of her stories was spartan and unromantic. The flat Midlands field-scape she called 'Lark Rise', after a local fieldname, was as different as it could be from the cosseting hills of Sussex.

Lynton Lamb, the illustrator of the first edition of the book, caught its personality with scraper-board exactness when he wrote that there was 'a queer quality about it, rather sinister, like the smell of wood-smoke from a gypsy encampment . . . it is the very low tone of the colour I think, the mole coloured thatch and the small trees like gorse'. Flora had somehow transmuted this subfusc settlement into another province of Deep England, whose self-reliant cottagers and their seem-ingly timeless traditions were the very stuff the country was fighting for.

The reviewers spotted this. The notices of the first two vol-umes were unequivocal about what made the books special, possibly unique, and mapped out a template for the way they would be perceived in the future. The first, *Lark Rise*, was pub-lished on the eve of war, and the *Saturday Review of Literature* saw qualities in it that the country was about to need again in spades. 'It is a vivid document, giving us the minutest details of the life of agricultural labourers in the 'Eighties. It also tells us something about the pride, dignity, and independence which underlay their impoverishment and their resignation.'

The *Manchester Guardian* agreed about its intimate authen-ticity and suggested that it was 'written with an insight that no mere spectator, however intelligent, could possess'. George

Dangerfield, in the *Saturday Review*, remarked on how the book was exceptional because it offered the minute details of life as seen by the villagers themselves, not 'through the windows of the Rectory'. The *Times Literary Supplement* talked of the author's 'reminiscences', and after praising 'the vivid memory and faithful portrait of a way of life that has almost passed', noted Flora Thompson's insistence on the contentedness of the villagers: 'if [her] memory is as good as it seems to be, they were neither unhappy nor dissatisfied with their lot'. All the critics concurred with the *Sunday Times*'s verdict that *Lark Rise* could 'claim the rank of an historical document'.

The second volume, *Over to Candleford*, was also warmly (if sometimes patronizingly) welcomed, and reviewers again accepted, unquestioningly, that it was both lyrical memoir and accurate social history, as if there could be no possible contradiction between the two. The *Spectator* noted that Flora had written of her childhood 'with that objectivity possible after long love, and a proud care not to romanticize'. 'An air of quiet enchantment broods over the narrative,' concluded the *Observer*, 'so artful is the concealment of art. This is rural England, unadulterated, fresh on the palate as summer lettuces or peas.' *Punch* thought that reading *Over to Candleford* was like looking out through a cottage window at a world of green tranquillity.

The critical reception was mirrored in the shops and both books became minor bestsellers. The war-weary public were hungry for portraits of what seemed like better times and for any glint of reassurance about their threatened cultural heritage. They wanted to know what it was like to go through privations and come out the other side. Above all – readers being inquisitive story-followers, even in wartime – they wanted to know what happened next to the enigmatic 'Laura'.

It's no surprise that in volume three, *Candleford Green*, Flora had chosen to recreate the period of her youth when she seemed happiest and most hopeful, working in a Post Office in the 1890s. The review in the *New York Herald Tribune* (the books were as successful in the USA as in Britain) described it as a worthy addition to the 'Candleford idylls' and predicted that Flora Thompson's 'delicately disguised autobiography' would become a valued documentary resource that would 'outlast current fiction in historical collections'.

When the combined edition was published in 1945, that year a perceptive review appeared in the *New York Times* by J. Donald Adams. He attempted to get to the marrow of the book, and explain its appeal. 'What Miss Thompson has done is to set down an autobiographical record of English village and small town life . . . She has done this with such particularity, and with such sharply remembered pictures of the people and the life which she knew as a child and young girl, that the parochial quality of her material is lost in its universality of appeal . . . "Lark Rise" is, in effect, Gray's Elegy made into a pageant that we intimately view. These are "the short and simple annals of the poor", but it is still a human life, without the degradation of the industrial slum . . . These books are not written in a nostalgic mood. There is no effort made to gloss over the hardness and narrowness of the lives depicted in them. Miss Thompson puts in everything that can give the picture life and truth. Nor does she moralize. I have never read anything that conveyed so poignantly the separation that lies between the state of happiness and what is known as progress.'

With such fair winds behind it, the *Lark Rise* trilogy settled down to become, in its small way, a national treasure. John Fowles (whose own fiction is noted for its games with memory) remarked of its author that 'Our literature has had no finer remembrancer in this [twentieth] century'. *Lark Rise* has spawned folk songs and plays and a branded range of furniture. The eminent cultural historian Raymond Williams dubbed it 'an irreplaceable record', and many academics began to regard it as a primary – and unimpeachable – source of evidence about rural life in the late nineteenth century. It was first included in Penguin's 'English Classics' series (including the introduction by Massingham) in 1973.

In the 1970s it became a set-book for some GCE English courses and was granted the ultimate plaudit of dedicated editions of Brodie's and Methuen's exam cribs. More sceptical than the 1940s' reviewers (though still regarding the book as memoir-cum-social history), the Methuen *Study Aids'* authors homed in on *Lark Rise's* possibly contentious sub-text. 'In what respects does Flora Thompson regard the way of life of Lark Rise villagers as superior to modern conditions?' reads one exercise. 'Do you agree with her? State your reasons clearly.'

The book (or perhaps the idea of the book) shows no sign of losing its charisma. Echoing the magnetism it had during wartime, *Lark Rise* has continued to surface like Excalibur during times of national economic distress; times when, as Flora wrote about the great agricultural depression, we were getting 'very near the bone'. In 1978, when Britain was deep in the 'Winter of Discontent' and Margaret Thatcher just a year away from declaring there was no such thing as society, Keith Dewhurst created a dramatized version for the National Theatre. It was staged in the round at the Cottesloe, with specially written songs and music by the Albion Band, a thumping political sub-text and cast and audience mingling as if they were in a street meeting.

Five years later, in the wake of the Falklands War and the

miners' strike, its patriotic and nostalgic potential were trundled to the front. *The Illustrated Lark Rise to Candleford* appeared in 1983, heavily abridged, and with the text interspersed with illustrations of flowers, Thomas Bewick cameos and reproductions of sentimental Victorian paintings by artists such as Helen Allingham. Sometimes the juxtapositions were jarring. An episode describing the forcible removal of a retired major to the workhouse faced Myles Birket Foster's *The Lacemaker*, a study of a 'happy family' group outside a picturesque cottage.

The illustrated edition was a publishing phenomenon, selling close on a million copies and remaining in the bestseller lists for thirty-one weeks. Three decades on, a hugely popular television adaptation coincided with the start of a major recession, and with the growth of interest in communitarian politics on both right and left, manifest in the ideas of the 'Big Society' and the Occupy movement. On television the feel-good aspects of Flora Thompson's text were again emphasized, and the four series which ran between 2008 and 2011 reached Sunday evening audiences of up to 7 million.

Yet this is where the status of the books becomes curious. The web of authorial legend and topographical curiosity that customarily builds up around nationally popular texts simply hasn't gathered around *Lark Rise*. Flora Thompson herself remains an almost invisible figure, known only from the hints she gave about her childhood in her own books. The patch of countryside she documented so minutely is an uncelebrated and largely unknown dot on the map. 'Lark Rise Country' hasn't become a coach-party destination. No tourists swarm around either its Oxfordshire motherlode, or the Wessex hills, a hundred miles to the west, where the action was relocated for television. The Timms family's old cottage, still a private house, is marked by a simple plaque, just visible through binoculars – the only evidence in the hamlet of Flora's, or the books', existence. It is as if, for all its exact description of a way of life in a precise locality at a specific time, *Lark Rise* has floated free from its physical moorings and its mortal creator and been absorbed into the amorphous, comforting mythology of Old England. The title alone – the journey from dawn chorus to candlelit evening – seems to act like a mantra, setting off poignant daydreams even in those who know nothing of the story that follows.

Underpinning *Lark Rise*'s eventful and sometimes incongruous history are two considerable and connected assumptions. The first is that Flora Thompson was a kind of *écrivain sauvage*, an untutored woman who discovered a gift for words late in her life. Flora Thompson's first biographer, Margaret Lane, may have been responsible for this notion, when she wrote that Thompson's 'strange' skill 'blossomed into fulfilment in old age', and did so 'without education or encouragement'.

The second assumption – that the books are strictly autobiographical and untainted by literary invention – sits comfortably with the first. Flora Thompson herself stressed that she had been imaginatively free with her characters and settings, so again an 'event' is dredged up to explain the assumption's origin. The publishers of the first editions, Oxford University Press, did not handle works of fiction in 1939 and Flora Thompson's books were 'reclassified' as autobiography to guarantee their publication. Ruth Collette Hoffman, in her literary analysis of Thompson's work, *Without Education or Encouragement* (2009) argues that this decision has warped interpretations of the book ever since.

But the label on the jacket is incidental. The perception that the book tells an essentially true story about a country child-hood springs from the character of the text itself, from its intimate detail and unadorned voice. It is hard to read *Lark Rise* and not *trust* Flora Thompson.

13. Encores

I began this short study finding myself most interested in how Flora Thompson's work fed from and contributed to our collective dreams of country life. I've come to its end more fascinated by her as an individual, an escapee from the rural working class and a self-taught writer who broke through the early twentieth century's considerable barriers for creative women. She appears as a person with complex unrequited longings, which she explored in a distinctive variety of fantastical non-fiction that seems to reflect the intense impression made on her by the prismatic landscapes of the south country.

But as a human being in every other sense she remains strangely impenetrable. I would love to have found out, for instance, whether, late in her life, she still spoke with an Oxfordshire accent, as she must have done in Juniper Hill; whether she was able to keep up her enthusiasm for chic fashion during the years of wartime austerity; how she translated her personal brand of conservative radicalism in the first post-war election of August 1945, which delivered a Labour landslide. These, alas, are not the kind of small, human details that Flora or anyone she knew bothered to put on permanent record.

But the writer and the private woman are the same person, and it was Flora's desire (or compulsion, even) to view her childhood memories through the lens of her complicated adult needs that lifts *Lark Rise to Candleford*, uniquely among her writings, from mere social history or memoir to a kind of fable. And it is the book's essentially fabulous nature that has allowed it to be reworked in new forms.

When, in 1978, the National Theatre staged its 'promenade performance' of a dramatized version of *Lark Rise*, it was in the wake of a similarly styled production of the Mystery Plays. In those productions, cast and audience had mingled freely in the open-plan arena of the Cottesloe Theatre, exactly as they must have done in open-air stagings of the plays in medieval times. Keith Dewhurst's adaptation of Flora Thompson's book used the same theatrical format, and scenes from *Lark Rise* transformed quite naturally into small morality tales. The whole play was set in the space of a single day – the first day of harvest – and used flashbacks (and occasionally flash-forwards) in a way that echoes the reminiscent tone of the book. In the Cottesloe production, Laura was an actor on the stage and Flora a disembodied voice-over. Jerry the fishmonger's homily about John Dories, the cheap-jack's sale of the tea-service, Twister's idleness, were played out as miniature parables, their 'framing' as episodes underlined by the Albion Band's music. The harvest itself was an astounding physical experience for the audience, with the harvestmen scything through them, as if they were a field of wheat.

When Bill Gallagher was invited by the BBC to devise and write a television adaptation of *Lark Rise to Candleford* in 2008, he also opted for the fable format. Beyond transporting the location from the sparse fields of Oxfordshire to the buxom hills of Wessex, the greatest liberty he took was to merge Candleford and Candleford Green. The action would revolve around a Post Office now situated in a hybrid market-town, and around a teenage Laura, who was in a position to take what seemed like weekly trips back home to Lark Rise. None of this, of course, was out of kilter with the freedom Flora herself had shown with place and time-frame. Beyond this, the series (more than forty episodes over four years) was loyal to the details and spirit of her text.

The formula was straightforward. Characters, incidents, customs and small details of food and dress were taken from the original text and freely scattered through the individual programmes. What Gallagher and the other writers added were strong storylines and character development, the two aspects of writing Flora had never mastered.

Few of the stories were taken from the books, and some were faintly ridiculous. (An ancient sampler embroidered with Adam and Eve – and with real human hair – is found on a grave, and becomes a kind of ink-blot test for all who see it.) But most catch the generosity and big-heartedness of Flora's books and a real sense of a rural world at a critical point of change. Developers threaten the landscape. Newcomers challenge the politics and habits of the old residents, not always for the worse. Inheritances briefly materialize and shine a spotlight on the real nature of poverty.

All these stresses are played out through the reactions of specific individuals and households. The reflective 'voice-overs' that are such a feature of Thompson's writing are given to Laura, who is writing them in her journal while her voice intones the words off-screen. The wisdom she shows is implausible for a teenager, but it enables her to end each episode with a small moral homily, a lesson learned.

One storyline in the very first episode encapsulates the adaptation for me. The Lark Risers are resentful of the fact that they have to pay 3s and 6d to have telegrams delivered to the hamlet, whereas Candleford gets them for free. It seems that this is because the Post Office has assumed that Lark Rise lies beyond the statutory distance limit for free deliveries. So Squire Timothy suggests that the distance should actually be measured, to settle the matter. What follows is a set-piece that would have done credit to Thomas Hardy – or John Ford. The great spool of rope, carried on a horse-drawn cart, is slowly unwound across the fields, accompanied by troops of people from both Candleford and Lark Rise, all dressed in their best clothes. It is a kind of beating-of-the-bounds, a ritual procession as well as an excuse for a picnic.

But there is also something brooding about the atmosphere, as Post Office officials, townees and villagers, squire and labourers, eye their different hopes at each other. In an offhand remark, Bill Gallagher once admitted that he saw Lark Rise 'as a Western', with settlers and strangers arguing about the values embedded in the land. It's an insight that, across a century, links Laura's vision of the hamlet 'as a fort' with Flora's achievement in setting out the framework of a kind of modern myth, in which that 'Western' spirit is still active. Today, the 'New Frontier' of development eats ever deeper into the countryside. Flora's villages have been stripped of all their neighbourly institutions. School, shop and Post Office have vanished. The Juniper Hill pub is now a private house, whose garden contains the region's last juniper bush, and the heath where they once grew in abundance is occupied by industrial agriculture all 'Over to Candleford'. Flora Thompson's exact and childlike vision of the generous economy of nature, and of the values of lives lived with the same inventive connectivity, has never been more relevant.

Sources

Primary sources: works by Flora Thompson

Bog-Myrtle and Peat, Philip Allan & Co., London, 1921.

Lark Rise to Candleford, OUP, Oxford, 1945.
Lark Rise (1939), *Over to Candleford* (1941) and *Candleford Green* (1943) were first published together under this title by Oxford University Press in 1945, with an introduction by H. J. Massingham. The Penguin Classics edition of 2008 has an introduction by Richard Mabey.

Still Glides the Stream, OUP, Oxford, 1948.

Heatherley, John Owen Smith, Headley Down, Hants, 1998.
This was not published in Flora's lifetime, but was found in the Flora Thompson archive at the University of Texas by Margaret Lane, and included in a slightly abbreviated form in Lane's collection of Flora's writing, *A Country Calendar and Other Writings*, OUP, 1979. Quotations in this book are taken from John Owen Smith's complete version, which he reset from the original typescript and published through his own company (John Owen Smith, Headley Down, Hants) in 1998, revised edition 2005.

Sources

The Peverel Papers: Nature Notes written in Liphook, Hampshire, 1921–1927, John Owen Smith, Headley Down, 2008.
Transcribed from the original articles in the Newspaper Library at Colindale by Ruth Collette Hoffman (see below) and John Owen Smith.

Biographical and critical works

Christine Bloxham, *The World of Flora Thompson Revisited*, Tempus Publishing Ltd, Stroud, 2007.

Ruth Collette Hoffman, *Without Education or Encouragement: The Literary Legacy of Flora Thompson*, Fairleigh Dickinson University Press, Madison, NJ, 2009.

Margaret Lane, 'Flora Thompson', an essay in the *Cornhill Magazine*, No. 1011, Spring 1957. Reprinted in *A Country Calendar and Other Writings*, OUP, 1979.

Gillian Lindsay, *Flora Thompson: The Story of the* Lark Rise *Writer* was first published by Robert Hale, London, 1990. Revised edition published by John Owen Smith, 2007.

John Owen Smith, *On the Trail of Flora Thompson: Beyond Candleford Green*, John Owen Smith, Headley Down, 1997. New edition published in 2005.

See also DVDs of the BBC television series *Lark Rise to Candleford*, which include comments by the writers, designers and producers.

Collections, archives

Harry Ransom Humanities Research Center, the University of Texas at Austin, where many of Flora Thompson's papers are held.

Oxfordshire County Record Office, Oxford.

Additional sources by chapter

Prologue

Gilbert White's *The Natural History of Selborne* was first published in 1788–9 and has been through more than 200 editions since. My biography, *Gilbert White*, appeared in 1986 (published by Century Hutchinson, London).

The late Anne Mallinson's presence in the village is caught in an exquisite short poem by Seán Street, entitled 'Selborne', in his collection *Cello*, Rockingham Press, Ware, 2013.

1. Juniper Hill: 'a gentle rise in the flat'

J. C. Blomfield, *History of the Present Deanery of Bicester, Oxon*, 8 vols, Parker & Co., Oxford, 1882–94.

Richard Davis, *A New Map of the County of Oxford*, engraved by John Cary, 1797.

Documents relating to the enclosure troubles are in the Oxfordshire County Record Office, Oxford.

See also Ruth Collette Hoffman, *Without Education or Encouragement*.

Sources

2. *Flora Timms: the awkward daughter*

Flora Thompson, 'A Country Child Taking Notes', *Readers' News*, 1947.

W. H. Hudson, *Far Away and Long Ago*, J. M. Dent, London, 1918.

3. *The Post-Girl: Flora moves on*

Thomas Wright, *Hind Head, or the English Switzerland*, Simpkin Marshall, London, 1898.

4 . *The Hilltop Writers: a spell in rural Bohemia*

Jan Marsh, *Back to the Land: The Pastoral Impulse in England, from 1880 to 1914*, Quartet Books, London, 1982.

Grant Allen, introduction to his book *The British Barbarians: A Hilltop Novel*, John Lane, London, 1895.

W. R. Trotter, *The Hilltop Writers: A Victorian Colony among the Surrey Hills*, new edn, John Owen Smith, Headley Down, Hants, 2003 (a comprehensive account of the growth of the Colony).

James Shirley Hibberd, *Rustic Adornments for Homes of Taste*, revised edn, London, 1856, CUP, 2011.

David Elliston Allen, *The Naturalist in Britain*, Allen Lane, London, 1976.

Charles Parnell, secretary of the Haslemere Microscope and Natural History Society, published *120 Years of Non-conformity in Haslemere* in 1908.

The Journals of George Sturt, 'George Bourne', 1890–1902, edited with an Introduction by Geoffrey Grigson, The Cresset Press, London, 1941.

5. *The* Fin-de-Siècle *girl*

Ronald Blythe, *Times Literary Supplement*, 23 November 1979.

6. *Writing as a Cottage Industry*

'Flora Thompson: Poet and Nature Lover', in *The Civilian* (Civil Service magazine), 14 May 1921.

Jonathan Rose, *The Intellectual Life of the British Working Classes*, Yale University Press, New Haven and London, 2001.

For Ronald Campbell Macfie's views on war, see 'Some of the Evolutionary Consequences of War', *The Lotus Magazine*, vol. 9, no. 1, October 1917.

7. *The Journalist: forest fantasies*

Daily Chronicle, 2 March 1921.

8. *The South Country: Flora and the sage of Selborne*

William Cobbett, *Rural Rides*, 1830; Penguin English Library edition, London, 1967.

W. H. Hudson, *Hampshire Days*, Longmans, Green & Co., London, 1903.

Edward Thomas, *The South Country*, J. M. Dent & Sons, London, 1909.

Sources

Gilbert White, *The Natural History of Selborne*, 1788–9; Penguin English Library edition, edited by Richard Mabey, London, 1977.

The Journals of Gilbert White, edited by Francesca Greenoak, 3 vols, Century, London, 1986–9.

Flora Thompson, *Guide to Liphook, Bramshott and Neighbourhood*, Bramshott and Liphook Preservation Society, 1925.

9. *The Making of Laura*

Flora Thompson, 'A Country Child taking Notes', *Readers' News*, 1947.

Stanley Baldwin, *On England and Other Addresses*, Philip Allan and Co., London, 1926.

Virginia Woolf, 'White's Selborne', from *The Captain's Death Bed and Other Essays*, Hogarth Press, London, 1950.

Judith Thurman, 'Wilder Women', *New Yorker*, 10 August 2009.

Raymond Williams, *The Country and the City*, Chatto & Windus, London, 1973.

Barbara English, '*Lark Rise* and Juniper Hill: A Victorian Community in Literature and History', *Victorian Studies*, 29:1, 1985.

Joseph W. Meeker, *The Comedy of Survival*, University of Arizona Press, Tucson, 1997.

10. Ballads and Bustles: Flora's folklore

Georgina Boyes, *The Imagined Village: Culture, Ideology and the English Folk Revival*, Manchester University Press, Manchester, 1993; new edition 2010.

Maud Karpeles, *Cecil Sharp: His Life and Work*, Routledge & Kegan Paul, London, 1967.

Linda Grant, *The Thoughtful Dresser*, Virago, London, 2009.

Juliet Dusinberre, 'The Child's Eye and the Adult's Voice: Flora Thompson's *Lark Rise to Candleford*', *Review of English Studies*, vol. 35, no. 137, February 1984.

11. War Work: the launching of the trilogy

Edward Thomas, *Richard Jefferies*, Hutchinson, London, 1909.

George Bourne [Sturt], *Change in the Village*, Duckworth, London, 1912.

F. R. Leavis and D. Thompson, *Culture and Environment*, Chatto & Windus, London, 1933.

W. J. Keith, *The Rural Tradition: A Study of the Non-fiction Prose Writers of the English Countryside*, University of Toronto Press, Toronto, 1974.

12. Celebrating England

Angus Calder, *The Myth of the Blitz*, Jonathan Cape, London, 1991.

Sources

Patrick Wright, *On Living in an Old Country: The National Past in Contemporary Britain*, Verso, London, 1985.

Alexandra Harris, *Romantic Moderns: English Writers, Artists and the Imagination from Virginia Woolf to John Piper*, Thames & Hudson, London, 2010.

Keith Dewhurst, *Lark Rise to Candleford: Two Plays*, Hutchinson, London, 1980.

Index

Index